THE
STUMP

Abridged Version
The Early Years

My Way Out of
Chicago's South Side

THE
STUMP

Abridged Version
The Early Years

CSM Terry L. Braddock
U.S. ARMY (RET.)
with Kathleen A. Braddock

Copyrighted Material

The Stump: Abridged Version – The Early Years

Copyright © 2017 by Terry L. Braddock. All Rights Reserved.

No part of this publication may be reproduced, stored in a retrieval system or transmitted, in any form or by any means—electronic, mechanical, photocopying, recording or otherwise—without prior written permission from the publisher, except for the inclusion of brief quotations in a review.

For information about this title or to order other books and/or electronic media, contact the publisher:
Terry L. Braddock
P.O. Box 1902
Boerne, TX 78006
www.thestumpmywayout.com
thestumpmywayout@gmail.com

Library of Congress Control Number: 2017913598

ISBNs: 978-0-9991516-0-0 (Hardcover Edition)
        978-0-9991516-3-1 (Paperback Edition)
        978-0-9991516-4-8 (Large Print Edition)
        978-0-9991516-5-5 (Abridged Edition)
        978-0-9991516-1-7 (eBook)
        978-0-9991516-2-4 (Abridged eBook)

Printed in the United States of America

Cover and Interior design: 1106 Design

Editor: David Aretha

Reprinted by permission from Cook County, Cook County Geographic Information Systems (GIS), image 2015408026, The Stump apartment building photo, p. IV and V. © 2017 Cook County Government.

Reprinted by permission from Cook County, Cook County Geographic Information Systems (GIS), image 2015406001, The A.O. Sexton Elementary School building photo, p. 3. © 2015 Cook County.

Reprinted by permission from Daniel Torres, author bio photo (back cover). Daniel W. Torres Photography.

FOREWORD

I KNEW AT A YOUNG AGE THAT MY city of Chicago was a place where anything and everything could happen, good and bad. But for me, an African American growing up in the '60s and '70s living on the South Side, there were more bad things happening than good. This is my journey of growing up in the ghettos of Chicago.

I suppose you think my story will be no different than a thousand stories you have heard or read before, normal American kids making our way. My story isn't just about a kid growing up on the South Side of Chicago; it's not about a kid who just wanted better; it's about a kid who simply wanted to save his life, to have a life, and I was determined to do just that. My story is different than so many others that have come before me — **I made it out.**

My hope in writing this story was to share how I made my way out of the ghettos of Chicago, and in doing so, show others with hard work and determination they can do the same. We all have choices in our life. The biggest challenge and hardest decision you will have to face in your life, is making the right choice. There will always be obstacles, barriers, and detours that will stand in your way when making that right choice; never stop believing in yourself, always follow your dreams.

The Stump

Some may ask why I titled the book *The Stump*. The Stump is what shaped and challenged me to become the soldier I was, and the man I am today. The Stump provided wisdom, direction, understanding, and motivation. It was a place full of love and sorrows, good times and bad, the place where my dreams were formed. The Stump prepared us for our lifelong journey to become men and women, and unknown to me at the time, it shaped me to see a brighter future . . . to realize I had a future.

It all started at the Stump — my way out.

CSM(R) Terry L. Braddock

The Stump. (Author collection)

TABLE OF CONTENTS

	Foreword	vii
1.	Duck and Cover	1
2.	The Greatest	7
3.	Mr. Dittle	11
4.	The Paper Route	15
5.	The Uniform	25
6.	The Dog	31
7.	Tennessee Summers	37
8.	Tennessee Summers cont'd	49
9.	Moving Objects	55
10.	A Touch of God's Hand	63
11.	The Baseball Game	69
12.	Hanging Out	73
13.	They Came Back	79
14.	The Sixth Sense	87
15.	Final Thoughts	93
	Notes	97

Chapter 1

DUCK AND COVER

The Cold War was quite frightening for a little kid who grew up during that time in our country's history. As a student in grammar school we periodically had bomb drills and they always scared me. My teacher would line us up in our classroom one behind each other and instruct us to walk single-file into the hallway; we were joined by the other students and told to stand against the walls. The teachers stood in the middle and yelled, "Everybody down." We fell to the floor, reached out, and covered our heads. This was constant throughout my early childhood years.

My grammar school (Park Manor Elementary School) was no different from any elementary school today; even back then we had bullies. Our school bully picked on kids smaller than he was and stole what little money they had. One day on the way to school the bully decided he was going to pick on me — that was a big mistake. I was not a kid he should have targeted for his attack.

He approached me and said, "Gimme your money," and at the same time he pushed me so hard I lost my footing and started to fall.

I've always had a quick temper and my dad (my stepfather) would tell me, "You need to think before you react." . . . But on that day, I certainly did not.

The Stump

My first school – Park Manor Elementary. (Author collection)

As my hand went out to break my fall it touched something hard, rough, and rectangular in shape. In that moment I was so angry and mad that I jumped up and hit him as hard as I could. I looked down and saw that I held a brick in my hand. The bully immediately fell to the ground and began to sob as blood poured out of the side of his head. I stood over him, brick in hand, and didn't move. I felt no emotion other than feeling so furious that he had knocked me down.

A teacher ran over and hollered, "Oh my God, what have you done?"

I didn't say anything. The principal came out and escorted me back to his office. The administrator called my parents, and sometime later my parents arrived. The principal told my mom and stepdad, "We cannot tolerate this type of violence. Your son has mental problems and we can no longer accept him at our school."

Duck and Cover

My parents had no other option — they were forced to move to another apartment, one that would be mapped to a different elementary school. I was expelled from the only school I had ever known, forced to leave my friends, and was enrolled in a different elementary school that, unfortunately for me, was in an even worse part of the city than where I had lived before.

My former school seemed pretty darn nice compared to my new one, which was old and in disrepair. What I experienced at my old school in terms of duck and cover during the bomb drills now became a routine occurrence for me, but in a different way...

We didn't have bomb drills like my first school, but we did have what is known today as drive-by shootings. Because of my temper and inability to control my anger, my parents were forced to move my entire family (to include my older sister and younger brother) to a different school district that had a lot of gang activity. Gangs drove around our

Second school – A.O. Sexton Elementary. (Reprinted with permission by Cook County)

The Stump

school, fired guns, and shot out our windows. For them I suppose it was fun, but for a young kid like me it was terrifying.

This was my new norm — my new duck and cover. When the teacher yelled, "Duck and cover," we dove under our desks and waited until the "all clear" was given when the bullets stopped coming. If windows were shattered, you would have thought they would have been replaced with new glass. Not at our school. They replaced them all right; but instead of replacing them with glass, they replaced them with plywood. We had more plywood windows than we had glass ones!

The plywood windows made the classrooms dark and claustrophobic. Even saying all that, the most damaging part of what happened to me during those duck and cover years was I saw no one from the local law enforcement community that seemed to care, not like they do in today's schools. The amount of shootings we had at our school, and the lack of any kind of law enforcement interest — more like "no interest" — became another item to put inside the Box (the place inside my head where I put my emotions).

Our schoolteachers were predominantly white, although the kids in my grammar school were all black. One would have thought my teachers would have been highly motivated in terms of our education and would have promoted learning and taught us how we could strive to do better. Not so at our school. What we got from them was just the exact opposite — as long as they got paid, they didn't care if we got a good education or not.

We did have a disciplinarian at the new school. In today's schools you would be sent to detention if you acted up, mouthed off, or did something you weren't supposed to do. In my school you were sent to Mr. Wright, our physical education teacher who was built like The Incredible Hulk. When you went to see Mr. Wright, he had what us kids called The Persuader, a huge wooden paddle with holes in it. Mr.

Wright didn't care what you did or didn't do; regardless, if you were sent to him you had a personal meeting with his paddle.

If you acted up you were sent directly to Mr. Wright, who was always in the gym. He'd take you over to the pummel horse that had two handles on top of it. You pulled down your pants and underwear, grabbed hold of the two handles, and your rear met The Persuader. The holes sucked the meat in. Mr. Wright got your attention! Today they would call that child abuse. For me it was more memories to put in the Box, and it is now part of my PTSD (posttraumatic stress disorder).

There was one saving grace with changing schools and moving to the ghetto; that was where I met Mrs. Hannaberry and found the Stump. Mrs. Hannaberry was a white woman, married to a black man. Interracial marriages were frowned upon in the '60s (and still illegal in sixteen states until 1967*), and by no means would suburbia be a place for a mixed-race couple to live. Mrs. Hannaberry's residence was the neighborhood meeting place. Soon after moving to the ghetto, my new childhood friends asked me, "Hey, man, do you want to check out the Stump?"

I asked, "What's that?"

One replied, "That's where Mrs. Hannaberry's at."

I paused a moment and looked at them thinking, *Who is Mrs. Hannaberry?*

They said, "She's real cool. You're really going to like her."

Thus began my journey to the Stump. My wife Kathleen once asked, "Did she have a house with a porch you sat on?"

I replied, "No, she lived in an old rundown apartment building that had long, crumbling concrete steps out front. That is where she always was; that was where all the kids in the neighborhood seemed to migrate to. Kind of funny: All those years I sat on those crumbling steps, I don't remember a lot of foot traffic coming in and out of that apartment building. Must have been God's saving grace we were left alone; alone and uninterrupted to learn from Mrs. Hannaberry."

Mrs. Hannaberry always had a stern look on her face. She wasn't big in terms of size — she was actually quite short. But what she lacked in size, she made up for in confidence. She was a straight-forward, tell it like it was woman. If she had something to say, she didn't mince words.

Mrs. Hannaberry always made sure we came to talk to her in those early years. You had to be prepared to read something to her, and she in turn would read to us. We practiced our spelling words, did our math problems, and she made sure our homework got done. Little did we know she had been an educator at one time or another in her life. Not so now; not living in the ghetto. We didn't know that at the time. She was just our Mrs. Hannaberry.

Chapter 2

THE GREATEST

One morning in grammar school (A.O. Sexton Elementary School — now closed) we were called to an assembly in our auditorium. As we lined up in our classrooms, moved down the hall, and took our seats with the stage in front of us, the principal came out and said, "Good morning, boys and girls. This is a great day for our school, and you are lucky to be part of this historical event. You will remember this day for the rest of your lives. You will be able to say, I was there."

He called a teacher to come forward and she began to call off kids' names. If your name was called you were to come up on stage. I heard my name being called and was surprised. I was happy but confused. I had no idea why my name was called but I made my way up on the stage as directed. I was pretty sure all the other boys and girls had the same thought I had. *Why were we all up here?*

We stood on the stage, side by side, all in a row, waiting to see what would happen next. The principal excitedly exclaimed like a circus barker, "They call him 'The Greatest of All Times,' even better than Joe Louis himself. Boys and girls, please join me in a big round of applause for the great — Cassius Marcellus Clay."

The Stump

As Mr. Clay came out on stage, the school erupted. I jumped up and down, clapped my hands, and cheered. There he was, on the same stage as me! Boy, was he big. He started at the end of the line, shook each and every one of our hands, and talked briefly to each kid on stage. He came closer and closer, coming down the line until it was finally my turn. How happy I was to meet someone of his importance.

As he reached his giant hand out to take my little one in his, he said, "Well, hello, young man, and what might your name be?"

I replied, "Terry Braddock, sir."

"Well, Terry Braddock, are you enjoying school?"

"Yes, sir."

"School is very important, isn't it?"

"Yes, sir."

"I want you to do something for me."

"Okay."

"I want you to stay in school, work hard, and get a good education; but more importantly, be somebody. Can you do that for me?"

I looked up at him with a big smile and said, "Yes, sir. Yes, sir, I can do that."

"Good young man."

He patted me on the back and went on to greet the next kid in line.

I was so excited the whole entire day, I didn't wash the hand he had shaken. I ran home when the last school bell rang and told my mom I had met Cassius Marcellus Clay. I told her not only did I see him, I shook his hand, and he talked to me too.

My mom said, "Did you enjoy meeting him?"

I said, "Yes, Mom, he's the greatest."

"Yes, son, he really is. What did he tell you?"

"Mom, he told me to stay in school, work hard, and be somebody. And Mom, you know what? I am going to do just that. I am going to be somebody."

Cassius Clay would change his name to Muhammad Ali in 1964.*

Chapter 3

MR. DITTLE

I SETTLED IN AT MY NEW SCHOOL, got good grades, kept up with my homework assignments, and interacted regularly with Mrs. Hannaberry. I might have been in the sixth grade the year when Mr. Dittle, my homeroom teacher, pointed to me as I stood up after the last bell rang and said, "Stop! Stay right where you're at." I sat back down in my desk. Everyone else had left, leaving just us two in the classroom.

Mr. Dittle was an old, crusty white guy. He walked over to me at my desk and I looked up at him and said, "Did I do something wrong?"

"No, you didn't do anything wrong."

I didn't understand why he had retained me after school. "Then why was I told to stay here?" I said. "I get good grades in class, I'm here on time, I'm behaving."

"Yes, you get decent grades in class, but I need you to understand something. I want you to continue to get good grades because those grades are going to get you the job I think you are worthy of someday."

"Mr. Dittle, I don't understand what you're talking about."

"I want you to picture this. My vision for you is . . . you are going to be responsible to lots and lots of people, maybe even hundreds of people." He got excited, clenched his hands together, and then spread

The Stump

out his arms like a preacher giving a sermon. "See the sign. In the middle of that sign, picture the word *custodian*. That's going to be you!"

All the air came out of my body. I was back at the Stump going over various spelling words with Mrs. Hannaberry. I remembered the meaning of that word.

I jumped up and said, "I don't want to be no janitor."

"Now, now, now, watch your words."

"No, I ain't going to be a janitor. I'm going to make something out of my life. I'm going to be somebody."

Again he said, "Now, now, now, you need to understand, you're a "N", and there's not a lot of opportunity for "N's". I'm just trying to set you on the right path."

Tears streamed down my face and I sobbed. "No, no!" I ran out of the classroom. I was so angry with him. I told myself, *I will not be what he wants me to be. I am better than that — so much better than THAT!*

I ran home, and as I stood in front of my own apartment building, all I could think of was I needed to talk to Mrs. Hannaberry. I turned and headed to the Stump; she was waiting for me as if she knew there was something going to be happening that day. She saw the tears that ran down my face and calmly said, *"What's wrong, Terry?"*

I cried out, "No, no," and pounded my fists on the concrete steps.

She put her hand gently on my back and said, *"Talk to me, Terry."* She then pulled out a handkerchief, wiped my face, and once again said, *"Talk to me."*

I told her what Mr. Dittle had said to me. A horrified look crossed Mrs. Hannaberry's face. She said, *"You are better than this. I have always had the best in mind for you. You are going to do better. Let no one tell you different. The first thing you must do is believe in yourself."* She looked at me and said, *"Do you believe?"*

In a muffled, soft voice, I said, "Yeah, I believe."

Mr. Dittle

She said, *"No. I'm not convinced. DO YOU BELIEVE? Give me that same anger you came here with. DO YOU BELIEVE?"*

All my anger Mr. Dittle caused me to feel came rushing back to me. In a loud voice I shouted, "I DO BELIEVE! I DO BELIEVE!"

"You will be okay. Look at me." She then said, *"You are going to make it. Give me a hug."* Mrs. Hannaberry squeezed me so tightly I could hardly breathe, and then she said, *"I am so sorry."*

I hugged her back and replied, "I'm better now."

I believe we don't remember the days; we only remember the moments . . . and so my time spent with Mr. Dittle in that classroom was one of my memorable moments, as memorable moments aren't always good ones. Everyone has moments in their lives. I call them "snapshots in time," but for me the days on the Stump were not only just "snapshots in time;" they will always be, for me, my most memorable memories of all.

Chapter 4

THE PAPER ROUTE

There's an old saying that goes, "If you treat people like animals then they will act like animals." I never heard that phrase used when I was a child. I doubt I would have understood the magnitude of what those words meant even though those words applied directly to me and to my surrounding environment I called home.

I did reflect on those words years later when I heard them as an adult, and I thought back to my schoolteachers and the police I encountered growing up on the South Side of Chicago. For me those two sets of social integrators, who were tasked to both teach and keep us safe, were the same men and women doing the most harm.

As a young black child, as a young black adolescent, and as a young black man, if your peers offer you no other assistance and guidance other than to call you a "N", and let you know the best you could ever become was a janitor, how could anyone expect you to succeed in life beyond those expectations?

If you didn't have caring parents and outside positive influences to impart self-worth, no wonder so many fell short by the wayside and failed to do anything with their lives. I was fortunate to have parents who wanted better for me and taught me the value of respect and self-worth, grandparents who were strong in their faith and provided that same continuous faith to me, and certainly Mrs. Hannaberry, who was my rock and guide not only for myself, but for so many others through our journey in life.

I now have a clear understanding of the meaning and importance of what that phrase really means. For anyone to succeed in life they need to be treated with dignity and respect, and in the end, this will lead a person to want to do better — rather than feel the need to do nothing, which eventually will lead to failure.

Every house and apartment in the neighborhood I grew up in had bars on the windows, and bars on both the front and back doors. Didn't everyone live with windows and doors that had bars on them? I, like every other kid in our neighborhood, thought that was the normal way to live. We weren't actually caged in our own homes, or it wasn't like we lived in a jail cell. There was one big difference — we had the freedom to come and go as we pleased. We had the keys to open up our locks anytime we wanted to.

All the stores in our neighborhood had bars on them too — grocery stores, shoe stores, restaurants, barbershops, hair salons, pool halls, and the liquor stores. This was the normal way of living for blacks in my community. No one ever questioned it; why would we? We never knew any other way. If a young black man got into trouble and was sent to jail, he seemed to adjust in jail better than others did; we had experience living behind bars. We were used to it. Everywhere we turned we saw bars. What's so strange about that?

My stepfather said, "This is not just security; this is a state of security. If someone wants to come in here, meaning our home, they are going to have to work for it."

We practiced how to lock ourselves in (both day and night), and how to unlock the locks to get out. It seems kind of strange that as a little kid I was taught the value of securing our home, but it was everyone's responsibility, not just adults. I'm not saying where I lived there were constant shootings, stabbings, muggings, or break-ins. I'm not saying that at all. What I am saying is you didn't want to encourage any of those things happening. It was our way of life; we learned how to secure our place of residence at a very early age.

One day our neighbor had visitors from out of town and I met an Italian kid. We decided to go play over at my house for a little bit, and as we approached my apartment building and reached our front gate, I saw a confused look on his face. My front gate had a lock on it. I unlocked it, we walked through it, and we quickly arrived at my front door, which also had several locks on it. He paused and asked, "Why do you have bars on your doors and so many locks?"

I replied, "To keep us secure."

"Don't you feel like a caged animal?"

For a brief moment I found myself speechless, but then replied, "No, I'm just like you; I'm not an animal. Maybe we just have a little bit more added security than you have."

"But why?"

"Because that's just the way things are."

We left it at that, with both of us trying to figure things out; one tried to understand why there was a need for so many locks and bars while the other wondered why he had been asked such a question and wondered whether he lived differently than the other little boy did.

I never thought about the possibility of fire breaking out or was scared of being trapped inside without a way to get out. My dad (stepdad) prepared us by having fire drills and ensured we all knew where the keys were located. My dad was smart; he hung a key rack directly on the wall to the right as you entered the front door. He had the hooks labeled with our name on it, and everyone knew where to hang their personal set of keys. He also had an extra set of emergency keys

The Stump

hanging on the key rack to unlock the door to get out in case of a fire or if an intruder got inside.

There was also a key rack hung by the back door as well. All the spare keys were located there, and that provided us with a second exit in case the front door was blocked. I bet his past military training helped him devise our escape plan; he sure drilled us like we were one of his soldiers. He would blow his whistle and say, "Everybody down. Move toward my voice."

My stepfather had joined the family when I was little. He was nothing like my biological father — he treated my mom with dignity and respect, and treated my older sister and me as if we were his very own. As a matter of fact, he always called me son.

After his time in the military, he became a professional painter in Chicago. He was six-one, weighed in around 200 pounds and had boxed in the Golden Glove. He was the kind of dad you were proud to be with!

Family was everything to him and keeping us safe on the South Side was his priority. When we practiced our fire drills he always told us to keep low because that is where the

My stepfather and mom. (Author collection)

oxygen would be. We practiced and crawled to the sound of his voice more times than I care to mention. We had it down pat; if something would ever happen to him, then my mom would take over and be in charge.

In my neighborhood everyone looked out for each other; you also looked out for your neighbor and your neighbor's property. You pretty much knew everybody who lived there and knew if someone or something was out of place. The South Side was full of three- and four-story brick buildings with numerous apartments inside; home for me was in one of these apartment buildings on the second floor.

I pitched in and had responsibilities at a young age and contributed as much as I could. I've never been afraid of hard work; I have always held a job even when I was a little kid. I got up each morning before I went to school and delivered the daily paper.

At 3:30 a.m. I was on my bike and rode it down to the paper company. Lots of other boys like me grabbed stacks of newspapers, including the *Chicago Sun-Times*, the *Chicago Tribune*, and the *Chicago Defender*. We rolled each newspaper, stretched a rubber band around it, and put it in our carrier bag.

We each had an employee number assigned to us that matched a number on a big board. Under our number was a hook from which hung what we called our D-rings. The D-ring was a metal ring that had tags hanging on it; each tag had the customer's name, address, telephone number, and which paper was to be delivered. Each paper had its own colored tag.

If you were a newbie at delivering papers, you counted the number of different colored tags to make sure you got the right number of each newspaper to put in your carrier bag. However, once you knew your route, you grabbed the papers that you needed and set out delivering, not even bothering to look at the D-ring, although you were required to carry it with you so the supervisors knew if you were on your route.

The Stump

The supervisors were pretty good about letting you know if you had any new customers to ensure you picked up extra papers to deliver to them.

My route was South Park Way, later renamed Dr. Martin Luther King Jr. Drive, following the 1968 assassination of Martin Luther King.* I rode and delivered my papers to various streets in our neighborhood before the customers got up to have their morning coffee. Once completed I rode back to the paper company to hand in my carrier bag and D-ring before I returned back to my home, leaving just enough time to get ready for school, have my morning breakfast, and head off to class.

We called Fridays collection day. That was when everyone had to go to each of the residences and collect the weekly fee for their paper. What tips we received we got to keep. I donated my tip money to my mom and dad; that was my way of helping out.

There was great risk involved on collection day. On the South Side of Chicago there was bad, and then sometimes there was really bad. We heard stories all the time about paperboys getting robbed. Every lowlife, thief, thug, and loser you could think of always knew when we were out collecting. There wasn't a Friday that went by that one or two paperboys didn't get robbed and sometimes even worse. During my years of delivering papers I was only held up one time. I was one of the lucky ones...

My dad taught us martial arts when he got back from Korea, which was one of his military duty stations he was assigned to. He reminded me often: "Think before you act, son. Sometimes it's not always wise to fight; it pays to be smart. Use your head when you are faced with certain situations."

On one Friday evening I finished up with my collections and came down a set of stairs in one of the apartment buildings. I noticed three guys standing on the outside of the building by the door. One stepped inside, walked toward me, and said, "What's up?"

The Paper Route

I looked at him and said, "What's up with you?"

"So what are you doing?"

"I think you know what I'm doing here."

He took a step closer to me and I saw a gun in his waistband. That made me think about what my father had said. *Think before you react.* If I reached for his gun, he could be faster than I was and grab it before I could get to it. Even if I did get his gun there were two other guys outside the door. My decision was pretty much made for me when the other two guys stepped into the apartment hallway and surrounded me in a semicircle.

"We can do this the easy way or we can do this the hard way — your choice."

I had maybe ninety dollars of collection money on me so it only took me a second to think, *Is your life worth ninety bucks?*

"Are you deaf? What's it gonna be?"

I said nothing and took out the ninety dollars.

"Now that's what I'm talking about. Show me the money."

I handed over the money, and the leader, who had been speaking the entire time, pulled his gun out and pointed it at me. He then pulled the trigger. Nothing happened; just a soft click. He replied, "This is your lucky day."

They all laughed and walked out of the building. I would never see them again. When I stared down the barrel of that gun, that barrel looked like the size of a cannon. Yet something happened that I couldn't explain. I had absolutely no feelings whatsoever; I was not fearful, nervous, or worried. I felt nothing. Shortly thereafter as I rode home, it didn't take long before the anger started to rage inside. I could definitely feel that.

When I got home I went straight to the punching bag my dad had hung for us and punched, kicked, and hit that bag so many times when I was done that I couldn't even raise my arms.

The Stump

The next morning I got up and prepared to go back in to get my papers for the Saturday delivery. No rest for the weary; no sympathy for the robbed! It was a common occurrence for at least one kid to be held up each Friday. Yesterday just happened to be my turn. No one ever got in trouble and you never had to pay back the collection fees — it was just an expense of doing business.

As I got up and moved around, I felt stiff and sore from punching the bag the night before. That reminded me of the reason I went after that bag so hard in the first place, and I thought it would be a good idea to take my dog with me on my route for added security.

My dog's name was Sheila, and we had gotten her when she was just a puppy. She was a German shepherd so we knew she was going to be smart, but from an early age she also acquired the strange habit of climbing trees. I kid you not. I don't know where it came from, but ever since she was little she was infatuated with trees. She learned to take her front paws, grip hard on the tree with her claws, and use her back legs to push herself up. Squirrels and cats didn't stand a chance around her.

The squirrels scurried around and taunted Sheila when she was outside; she, of course, would chase after them. The first thing they did was run up a tree thinking that was going to be the safest place they could go; boy, were they wrong. Up she went, scaring them to death. You had to be there to see it. Depending on how thick the tree branch was she would even walk out on the limbs. Nowhere was safe when Sheila was outside.

Fences didn't stop her either. She had springs like a gazelle and would hop right over them like they weren't even there and wander around the neighborhood, but she always knew how to get back home. She was very smart and was a special dog from day one.

Saturday morning after the robbery I let Sheila run along beside me. I got my papers, prepared them, and off we went delivering them to everyone's home. We came to an apartment building where the delivery was made in the back of the building. It had a spring-loaded gate that snapped closed instantly once you released it. I opened the gate and went in, and as I launched the paper to the second floor landing, a sharp and intense pain shot across the middle of my back. It was so painful that it knocked me to my knees.

I laid there and tried to catch my breath. I thought maybe I had just turned wrong and the pain would go away after a couple of seconds and then I'd get up. I thought I'd be okay, but it didn't work out that way. The opposite happened. It got worse. Sheila hopped the fence that had closed behind me when I fell to the ground, ran over to me, and began to whine. I said, "Go home. Bring help."

She looked at me, cocking her head to the left and right to try to understand what I was saying.

I said again, "Go home. Go!"

She turned, jumped back over the fence, and took off down the alley at a full sprint. It seemed like an hour or more but probably was only about thirty minutes before Sheila brought my dad back. My dad explained that Sheila had come to the back door, barked, jumped up and down, would run away, bark, come back, run away, bark, and come back. He figured something must be wrong because he knew she had gone with me on my paper route. My dad followed Sheila and she brought him right to me. It turned out I had muscle spasms all across my back — nothing a heating pad and rest wouldn't take care of.

A click away from losing your life would stress anyone out. That and pounding on that punching bag until I was exhausted the night before didn't help either. I'm sure all of that had an impact on me getting back spasms, but I had youth on my side and recovered quickly. Sheila got a big fat treat that day; and for me, it was just another day in the life of a ghetto kid.

Chapter 5

THE UNIFORM

ONE OF MY FONDEST MEMORIES of my father (my stepfather) was when I saw him in his military uniform. Time had passed and my mom had remarried. I called my stepfather "father" or "dad," as I've always considered him to be both of these.

The sight of him in that Army uniform made me proud and greatly influenced the direction I eventually chose to take as an adult. I had no doubt in my mind, even at an early age, that I wanted to be a soldier. Usually if your father was in the military or if you had family members in the military, you were encouraged to go that same route in life. My father was different. I remember he wanted one and only one thing for us. He wanted us to get an education; everything else was secondary. I, however, wanted to be a soldier, from day one.

My stepfather during the Korean Conflict in his Army fatigues. (Author collection)

25

My great uncles in WWII serving in the Navy and Army Air Corps. (Author collection)

When my friends and I played pretend (girls called it dress-up), they always played cops and robbers or were firemen, doctors, or lawyers. I always chose to be a soldier. One day when I was at the park, I saw a group of kids in blue uniforms at a distance. I didn't know what or who they were. I could see they had some kind of scarf around their necks and what looked like a ring around it about chest high. It somehow pulled the scarf up and parted it into two pieces.

I asked a grown-up who stood near me, "What are they?"

The grown-up said, "They are Cub Scouts."

My sister serving in the Air Force during the Vietnam Conflict and after. (Author collection)

I stood and looked at them; seemed like forever until they walked out of my sight. I ran as fast as I could home to my mom, who was in the kitchen cooking, and in an excited voice I exclaimed, "Mom! Mom!"

Thinking something was wrong because I was out of breath and all worked up, thinking I had hurt myself, she said, "What's happened?"

"I want to be a Cub Scout!" She paused and said, "You want to be what?"

"A Cub Scout!"

She looked at me and said, "I don't have time for this — go away."

I wasn't to be deterred and said again, "I want to be a Cub Scout, Mom."

She stopped what she was doing and said, "Come with me."

She took me into the dining room, pulled out the yellow pages, and said, "Hum." After studying more of the pages in the phone book, she closed it and said, "I got work to do. Go outside and play."

I looked up at her and felt sad because I thought she didn't want to talk about it anymore. What I didn't know was when she had looked

The Stump

in the yellow pages that day, there weren't any Cub Scout dens in our area. Not surprising; we did live in the ghetto.

My mom was a determined woman who cared deeply for her children. She was strict and firm with all of us, and although her life was far from easy, she always managed to have a smile on her face. That smile along with my mom's pretty face, got her modeling jobs when she was young. And although she wasn't very tall, as small and petite as she was, she always held her own — she is an intelligent and confident woman, who always told us to never half-step in life. Always give it your best.

My mom the model. (Author collection)

The Uniform

And so she later set to work and searched for the closest Cub Scout den to our ZIP code. It took her a couple of days but she did find one; it was clear across town. She signed me up, and between her and my dad they managed to get me to the scout meetings on the scheduled days. When they were both tied up and couldn't drive me, I took public transportation — caught two buses all by myself. My mom practiced with me and made sure I knew how to catch the right bus. She made me familiar with the transfers I needed to make to get to my meetings on time.

What a proud day when I got my Cub Scout uniform. I had brought home the flier with the order information on it and gave it to my parents. I'm not sure how they swung paying for the uniform — it wasn't like we had any extra money to spare — but they got it ordered up for me. Somehow they made it work. They always managed and found a way to support all of us kids. I was so excited when the uniform arrived that I wore it to school that next day.

From that day on I've always had a uniform to wear. After the Cub Scouts I became a Boy Scout, then later joined the JROTC program in high school. I knew that was my calling. I wanted it so badly and worked so hard. As I entered my senior year of high school, I achieved the highest rank in the JROTC program; I became the battalion commander (lieutenant colonel) of our high school JROTC cadets.

There was no doubt in my mind I was destined to be a soldier

Proud to be in a uniform – Boy Scout and JROTC. (Author collection)

The Stump

in the United States Army. After my high school graduation, I began my thirty-seven plus years in the military. I achieved the highest enlisted rank of E-9 and attended the most prestigious school an enlisted soldier can attend — the United States Sergeants Major Academy — and wore the rank of Command Sergeant Major.

Chapter 6

THE DOG

We didn't have school buses on the South Side like the white neighborhoods did. I had the pleasure to walk to school every day. I passed one particular house each morning that had a chain-link fence that kept a bulldog at bay. Don't get me wrong; I like dogs and have one myself now. But I gotta tell you, this particular bulldog was mean in spirit and ugly as all get out with that smashed-in looking face. God must have made the bulldog on the sixth day and ran out of ideas for beautiful creatures. Either that or he was getting tired and threw something together fast before saying, "Done!"

It seemed like this bulldog only had an issue with me. Other kids walked past and he wouldn't bark. Lazy-butt just sat there. Not in my case. This bulldog hid and tried to catch me off guard. I didn't understand what his whole motive was. Stupid dog waited just for me, and even though I was in the seventh or eighth grade at the time and knew he was going to be a butt, he always managed to surprise me.

The bulldog would charge the fence, snarling at me like he wanted to take my head off. When he got the drop on me, a smirky smile came across his face like he was pleased with himself. He didn't have a real tail, just a stupid stump of one he'd wag back and forth. After being

The Stump

surprised yet another morning, I thought, *Okay, it's time — something has to change*. I needed a plan and set about thinking about one.

Later that same day I was with a few of my partners playing basketball at the park. We got thirsty and walked over to the corner store, bought a Coke and a bag of chips, and walked back to the courts. As we rested I watched a little boy playing on the slide. Our park had two aluminum slides that were positioned right next to each other — one short one and a real tall one. They were the shiny metal kind that blinded you when the sun bounced off of them, and were also the ones you burned your legs on and stuck to when going down them on hot days.

The kid was no more than four or five, and he'd been going down the smaller of the two slides by himself the entire time we were taking a break. His mom held a baby girl in her arms and watched as he went up and down.

I saw him point to the larger slide, and his mom nodded yes. He walked over and stopped at the bottom of the steps. He looked up, must have gotten scared, and turned to his mom. I figured he asked his mom to go up with him because she paused for minute, sat the baby girl on the grass, walked over to her son, and with his mom directly behind him, he climbed up the steps and shot down the big slide with his mom following right behind him.

In the meantime, the baby girl who had been placed in a sitting position on the grass had tipped over and started crying, unable to sit back up on her own. The mom ran over, picked up the little girl, and hugged and kissed her. The little boy wanted to go down the big slide again, and the mom gestured for him to go it alone as she was busy trying to get his little sister to stop crying. The little boy walked over to the big slide and looked up at the steep steps. He paused, walked back over to his mom, and tugged at her arm as if he wanted her to come and climb up the stairs with him again as she had the first time.

She pointed to the slide, and I can imagine she must have said something like, *You can do it — I know you can. You went up those steps and down the slide just fine the first time — I didn't help you one little bit. You did it all by yourself, remember? It's only your fear that is stopping you from having fun . . . take a deep breath and climb those stairs. I know you can do it.*

He walked back over to the tall slide, looked up at the steps, and looked back over at his mom. She nodded to him, and with her index finger she pointed up the stairs as if to say, *Go!* I could see he struggled with wanting to go up the stairs but was scared to take that first step. He finally grabbed the side handles and made his way up the steps. He sat his little butt at the top, paused for just a moment as if to savor his accomplishment, and down he went, a big smile plastered on his face. His mom met him at the bottom and gave him a big hug.

After that there was no stopping him, and he was still going up and down that big slide when my partners and I started playing ball again. I left early from the park ahead of my partners; my mom was cooking dinner and I needed to get home. I walked by myself, thinking about how that little kid had conquered his fear of the big slide. It got me thinking about that bulldog, and I wondered why he only barked at me on the way to school, and no other kids. Somewhere I had read that dogs could sense if you were scared. I wondered deep down if I was afraid of that bulldog and that was the reason he always messed with me.

After we ate I went into the living room and pulled out the "D" *Britannica Encyclopedia* (an old person's book version of the Internet for any young readers who do not have a clue as to what an encyclopedia is). I took the cream-colored book trimmed in dark green, embossed with gold lettering on the front, and set it on the dining room table. My mom asked me what I was working on, and I said I had to write a paper for school. That encyclopedia set, along with the children's book version, was our main resource for completing research for school. Our family was privileged to have an encyclopedia set, as they were pricey. When the salesman had come to the house, my dad told my mom it was a must-have. When it came to anything dealing with a better education, he was all-in. Half the neighborhood or more used our set of encyclopedia books to complete their school papers.

I turned the pages until I came to the chapter on dogs, saw the different breeds listed along with their pictures, and located the bulldog. It stated they were wonderful with children — not from my perspective, but again, maybe the problem was with me more than the bulldog. I read about how to train a dog, and a plan started to form in my head.

I waited until it got dark and then set out through the alley. I didn't want any witnesses to take note of what I was about to do. Going into someone's yard at night isn't a good idea on the South Side — that's something that could get you shot. My night was either going to end up good or real bad, but either way I was going to address my problem.

I left the back alley, cut to the front, and reached the yard with the chain-link fence where the bulldog lived. He was lying down and looked to be asleep, so I whistled at him. I took an Oscar Mayer hot dog out of my pocket and broke off a small piece. He realized it was me, the one he loved to torment, and charged the fence — ready to act his usual crazy until he saw I had food in my hand. He changed his mind about acting stupid when I stuck the piece of the hot dog through the fence and it fell on his side, where he quickly gobbled it up. I kept tearing off little bits of the hot dog and poked them through the fence until he had downed the entire hot dog.

It was no big deal feeding the bulldog with the fence between him and me. No sweat, but I knew I had to face the bulldog man to man. I told him to stay, had no idea if he knew what that meant, and took off and went around to the backyard, which had a wooden fence. (The chain-link portion was on the front side, facing the street where the sidewalk was.)

The Dog

I tossed a softball over the fence into the bulldog's yard. The "Chicago-style" softball was oversized, played barehanded, and was used throughout the entire city and suburbs. My plan B if the dog bit me was to say my softball went into the backyard and I jumped the fence to get it. I scaled the back wooden fence and jumped down on the other side, praying the bulldog wasn't going to run up and bite me.

The bulldog really didn't seem to care if I was inside his yard or not. His only concern was that I share the second hot dog that I pulled out of my pocket. I knelt down and put a piece of hot dog on the grass and let the bulldog eat it that way. For the next bite I left it in my hand and he gently took it from my fingers. Now the big test — with the hot dog in one hand, I reached and petted him with the other. He didn't pay me no mind, just ate the hot dog. He finished up the second hot dog, which was all I had brought with me, allowing me to pet him the entire time.

For a fleeting second I thought I should have saved one last piece to throw away from the fence so I could run and get out of his backyard. Too late for that, so I showed the bulldog my empty hands and he set about to lick them, getting every last drop of hot dog juice. He finished up, I petted him a few more times, walked over and picked up my softball, threw that back over the fence into the alley, stepped on the bulldog's doghouse (which sat next to the fence), and hopped back over. I found my softball and then went around to the chain-link fence and he came right over. He licked my hand once again, and I left to go back home. Mission accomplished.

Next morning when I walked to school, I paused as I passed by the bulldog's house. He ran over to the fence and I was ready with a piece of bacon I had saved from breakfast. We seemed to have an understanding now, and from that day on he never growled at me again.

As I continued on to school, I remembered Mrs. Hannaberry tell us, *"We all have to face our fears someday and all of us have different*

The Stump

demons. The day will come that you have to make a choice: to continue to be frightened for the rest of your life, or stand up to what you are afraid of. It won't be easy — life never is — but if you face your fears with the inner strength we all have inside, you will prevail, and be a better and stronger person for it."

Chapter 7

TENNESSEE SUMMERS
(The Top)

My summers were spent in Tennessee at my grandparents' farm. Most kids couldn't wait for that last class bell to ring that signaled school was done for the year and summer break had finally arrived. Time to sleep in, goof off, and play basketball all day until your mom called you in for supper. That wasn't my summer. My summer was only one thing — work. Hard work! My summers were spent in the cotton and pea fields of Tennessee, drenched in sweat.

I couldn't have been more than six or seven years old when we started going down south to spend our summers, but I was old enough to help out, and old enough to see that another world existed outside of the city life of Chicago. My brother, sister, and I were loaded up in the car, and off we headed to Grandma and Grandpa's house. That was on my mom's side — her parents.

I saw a lot of differences between my city and that small southern town of Macon, Tennessee. It actually wasn't even technically a town; it was an unincorporated community in Fayette County located just east of Memphis and sat just north of the Mississippi border. The town

The Stump

My grandparents' house in Tennessee – front and back views. (Author collection)

maybe had a population of 1,000 people, if that. Heck, my school in Chicago had more kids in it than that whole entire town had. There wasn't much in downtown Macon either. If you drove slowly you could get through town in five minutes. Back in Chicago you could drive for miles and see nothing but street after street, and highways built on top of highways.

Not so in Macon. It had only one major road and that was named Main Street. Chicago was so big they ran out of names and started using numbers — just easier that way. Macon had one gas station with a little coffee shop in it, one grocery store, and one ice cream parlor with candy in it. Up on a little hill sat a little white pristine church (only whites were allowed to enter, even in the '60s). That was all there was to that little town.

Macon and the surrounding area did have one thing that Chicago didn't. They had Mr. Charlie's House. As we neared Macon, in the distance you started to see beautiful houses set back from the road, spaced far apart, with white fences, and fields with horses in them. There was nothing but acres of land surrounding these noble houses. We didn't have anything like that in Chicago. I called them the "Big Houses." My grandmother used to say, "That's Mr. Charlie's House."

I asked her, "Who is Mr. Charlie, Grandma?" Clearly, this wasn't during the time of slavery. The summers I spent in Tennessee were in the '60s and early '70s, but that is how my grandmother and grandfather described the white plantation owners of those huge houses with their acres and acres of land that surrounded them. Mr. Charlie owned them.

My grandfather worked at the cotton gin right there in Macon. He was one of the old Tuskegee Airmen in the Army Air Corps and got that job when he came out of the service. He worked in that cotton

The Stump

The occasional visit from my grandparents to Chicago (Grandma, Mom, Sister, Brother, me, Grandpa, and Sheila as a puppy). (Author collection)

gin for many years before it finally closed. A short and stocky man, he was good with his hands and he could fix anything — he used that skill when he was a mechanic in the Army Air Corps. He smoked and he drank, but that was just the way it was back then. Working from sunup to sundown, he was well known and admired as a man who would give you the shirt off his back; if he thought you needed it.

He and my grandmother owned a farm seven miles out of town. It wasn't much to look at, just a small, ratty-looking place with a few cows, pigs, horses, and chickens. He planted peas and cotton as his main crops, and if you were old enough to pull a bag, you were old enough to be out in the fields working! I was a gloried pea picker, and when that crop was harvested, I became a gloried cotton picker.

I have clear memories of picking cotton even though I would have been pretty young at the time. Those memories I can recall perfectly. I pulled cotton off the vines that had leaves on them that were razor sharp, sharp enough that they cut your hands. You didn't stop, though; there wasn't time for breaks. You picked and put the cotton in your bag until it was full, then you dragged your bag to a wagon with a big scale on it. A grown-up would lift your heavy bag up, weigh it, and, based on the weight of the cotton you had picked, that is how much you — well, Grandpa — got paid.

That was backbreaking work. I had looked at the rows and rows of cotton that seemed to go on forever, knowing all of it had to be picked, and thought there was no way we were ever going to get all of that done. There wasn't a lot of work for blacks in town. They farmed and relied on what they grew, what they took to market to sell, and what they brought back from the market to meet their daily needs. Farming was their way of life and became my way of life during the summer.

My grandma had a big garden, and that was where the produce came from that was sold at the market. She grew tomatoes, okra, and watermelon, and she had what she called a mustard dime tree. My grandfather had a cornfield he planted, but he didn't have any of the modern-day tools to cultivate the land. He worked it with a plow strapped to a horse and a mule that pulled it through the field. The soil was turned over and got the field ready to replant the next growing season. His hands were cut from holding on as he gripped the plow. It all was backbreaking work. It seemed to me, everything we did on that farm required good old-fashioned, all-American hard work.

Every now and then sometimes at night, my grandpa and my uncles would get together to slaughter hogs. They would start a big bonfire,

The Stump

kill the hogs, skin them, and cut the meat up. My grandmother would make crackling bread and give us kids the fried skin to eat; I think they call them pork rinds today. That was good eating.

In the evenings when I was done with work in the fields, my grandmother would sit me by a big pottery-type bowl that stood three feet high. It had a lid with a hole in the middle of it. A stick came out of the hole, and I would push that stick up and down. Eventually I churned the milk so much that by the time I was through and took the lid off, I had fluffy, white, creamy butter to give to Grandma. There was also milk left over that didn't turn to butter, and Grandma poured it out for us to use as our buttermilk.

We used to get so happy when Grandmother said, "You want some milk and bread?" That meant fresh-baked homemade cornbread, sliced open with melted butter wedged inside, and then warm buttermilk poured on top. That was the best eating we ever had as a kid. The taste of that bread with the home-churned butter and buttermilk coming through the bread, the way it just melted in your mouth, that was heaven.

I must admit we ate well down south, better than in the city. Grandma and my aunts made fried chicken, collard greens, and black-eyed peas, and for dessert someone walked down to the garden and picked a fresh watermelon. That didn't happen in Chicago. But even saying all that, nothing was as good as Grandma's milk and bread! That was the best.

Grandma bought the big cans of stewed tomatoes and butter beans at the grocery store to cook with — the large commercial-sized cans. She gave us the lids from the tops to play with, and we used them as Frisbees to throw around. Kathleen stopped me as I told her this story and asked, "Weren't they sharp?"

I answered, "I guess they were, but we were kids and didn't know any better. We threw them in the air, ran around, had fun with them; they were our Frisbees."

One Sunday, we kids were out playing with our tops and they all landed on the roof. There were perched right there on top of the house, and there they stayed. They wouldn't move; they were stuck. My sister and brother ran over to the house, fell to their knees, and started to pray. I walked over and looked down at my brother and sister and thought, *That's never going to work.*

It wasn't but a minute later until my sister's top flew down and then my brother's top followed. Both tops had blown off the roof and landed on the ground right beside them. I looked at them, looked at my top still stuck on roof, and then looked at my grandmother, who had come outside probably because it had gotten quiet when we stopped running around making noise. She probably wondered what we had gotten into.

She looked at me and I looked up at my top still stuck on the roof. I hurriedly said some hasty words as my prayer offering, and my grandma softly said, "Come here, Grandson."

I walked over to her and she had me sit with her on the porch. She said, "You have to believe, Grandson. Until you truly believe you are never going to be saved and your prayers will never be answered. You do not believe, do you? You aren't a believer? We need to go to church, but I want you to do something for me first."

"What's that, Grandmother?"

"Go in the house and write a letter to God."

"What?"

"Go do what I told you."

I went inside the house and went to my bedroom, sat down, and thought to myself, *I don't know how to talk to God. What am I supposed to say to him? I don't know what to write.*

I picked up a pencil and wrote, "God, I don't know what I'm supposed to say but my grandma told me to write a letter to you. If you're listening I'm about to go to church with her so if you don't mind, if you can find it maybe in your heart to bring my top down, I'd really appreciate it. Thank you."

I folded up my note and put it under my pillow.

Off I went to church with my grandma, who told the pastor, "My grandson needs to be saved."

To me she said, "When it hits you, you will know."

I said, "Know what, Grandma?"

She said, "You're a hardhead. You will know; you will know when it happens."

"Okay, Grandma."

I didn't know what she was talking about, but they made me sit down in the front pew. The pastor ranted away, worked up a sweat, and I suppose he delivered a powerful message; must have been because as he preached those mighty words he got to jumping around, up and down. He eventually came over, stood over me, and yelled, "Do you believe in God?"

I looked at him and thought, *I'd better say yes or else he and Grandma would chew at me and yell at me some more.* I hurriedly replied, "I believe, I believe."

He said, "Do you believe in Jesus Christ, The Glorified Heavenly Father? Do you believe? Do you believe?"

I once again hurriedly replied, "I believe, I believe."

My grandmother jumped up somewhere behind me and yelled, "NO, HE DO NOT!! NO, HE DO NOT!!"

I thought to myself, *Oh God, here we go.*

I said, "Grandma!"

She came down front, grabbed me, and yelled, "YOU ARE NOT SAVED. GET DOWN ON YOUR KNEES. ASK FOR FORGIVENESS. RIGHT NOW, GRANDSON, RIGHT NOW."

My grandma grabbed me out of the pew, slammed me to the floor, and as she spoke those words she pressed her hand to my back. I have never felt anything so strong in all my life. My grandmother's hand felt like the Lord himself holding me, and I couldn't move. I was in a trance, and something happened but I don't know what it was.

Next thing I knew someone pulled me up off the floor. I was hot, sweaty, and all out of breath. My grandma said to the congregation, "Lord, praise God, this boy is saved. He is so saved."

To me she said, "You are so saved, Grandson!"

Stunned, I said, "What do you mean, Grandma? What happened?"

She said, "You ran around inside this church with your hands up, waving them around and around. I just knew the Holy Spirit had you, and He was the one that moved you to run around this church."

I didn't recall any of that. I asked Grandma, "I did that?"

"You did more than that, Grandson. You were saved. The pastor blessed you and saved you. You are saved, you are saved."

I was so happy and excited when we got home after church that I jumped out of the car and ran to the house thinking surely my top must be on the ground. I ran around the yard and thought my top had to be on the ground somewhere; it had to have blown off the roof when I got saved. It never occurred to me to look up; it couldn't still be on the roof of the house.

My grandma said, "Grandson, what are you doing?"

I said, "Grandma, you said I was saved, right?"

"Yes."

"Then, Grandma, where's my top?"

She looked up, pointed, and said, "It's still on the roof."

"But you said I was saved."

"Grandson, just because you were saved don't mean that God heard your prayer. He saved your soul but he still hasn't heard your prayer."

I walked around and thought about what my grandmother had said and finally dropped to my knees and really prayed. I had never prayed like that before in all my life. I stayed on my knees until a sudden

The Stump

gust of wind came out of nowhere. It moved my top off the roof and landed it right down beside me. I got up real slowly and looked at the top laying on the ground. I stood there for a moment, reached down, picked it up, looked up at the sky above, ran into the house, and yelled, "Grandma, Grandma!"

I showed her the top and she said, "I think the Lord heard your prayer. Yes, he did."

My grandmother always had a smile on her face — I never remember seeing grandma without one (other than when she was using the switch on me). She was also a big hugger, and loved to kiss us on our cheeks. A churchgoing and God-fearing woman, she was dedicated to her religion.

My grandma wasn't well educated, but she was smart in her own way. She always told me I was the hardheaded one out of the bunch. Problem with that was I knew she was right. I got a lot of spankings from her too; I always seemed to be in trouble for one thing or another. When I got older I'd take off like a heartbeat when Grandma thought I needed to be taught a lesson. I overheard her tell my aunt, "That boy is fast — he's so fast. That boy can run."

When I was younger she'd tell me, "Go out there and get me that switch." When I was real little I didn't understand what was going to happen so I'd go out and get a switch and bring it back to her. Grandmother would pull most of the leaves off but leave a few at the tail end, and she'd whoop me with it. As I got older and wiser I began to realize, *That's stupid helping to bring Grandma what I'm going to get hit with — I'm not going to do that anymore. I'm not going to get the switch.*

Sometimes I am asked what do I remember the most about a certain loved one in my family. I always remember my grandmother's last words to me before she died. They have stuck with me all these years . . .

Twenty-four hours before I took my final exams at the Sergeants Major Academy, my mom called to let me know that Momma Doll-Baby (my mom's nickname for her mom) was up in Chicago visiting her and she was going to take her to the hospital for a checkup. My mom said Momma Doll-Baby wanted to speak to me.

Grandma said, "Grandson, your momma got me up here (in Chicago) and she wants to take me to the hospital to get checked out."

Concerned, I said, "Grandma, are you okay?"

"Let's just say she wants to make sure I'm okay. But I want to tell you something."

"What's that?"

She continued, "I'm going to the hospital but I won't be coming back."

I interrupted, "What are you talking about, Grandma? She's just taking you to the hospital to get checked out."

"Listen to me, Grandson, listen to me. I don't have much time. I want you to listen."

"Okay, Grandma."

"I want to leave these words with you: Whenever you have a problem, no matter how big or how small it is, I want you to give it to the Lord and leave it alone."

She didn't say anything else and gave the phone back to my mom. That was the last thing she ever said to me. My grandmother went to the hospital that evening and passed away.

Chapter 8

TENNESSEE SUMMERS CONT'D
(Two Worlds Collide)

My summers spent in the South came to an abrupt end when I was sixteen years old. As I matured throughout my teenage years, going to Tennessee for the summers became a challenge for me. I began to identify differences in how blacks were treated in the South, compared to how they were treated up north in Chicago.

Down south my grandfather and grandmother never looked a white person in the eye. They never raised their eyes to them at all, either when spoken to or if they passed a white person on the street. They even went so far as to tell me never to look at, or speak to, a white girl. I learned the rules early on, and the swing was pretty simple in Macon. When you talked to anyone white — didn't matter if it was a white woman, white man, or even a white teenager — you always looked away and down.

The Stump

There were a lot of words or phrases spoken by the whites to my grandparents that made me uncomfortable, the words *boy,* *"N",* *you,* or a combination of, "Hey, I'm talking to you, boy!"

These were all words that haunted me. Back home in Chicago sitting on the Stump with Mrs. Hannaberry, she had taught us these words were disrespectful, and if someone addressed us in such a fashion, the person who spoke these words did not respect us as a person. I was taught to show respect to everyone, black or white. That was how we rolled up north.

I began to question my grandparents more and more and asked why they allowed themselves to be spoken to in what I viewed was in a disrespectful way. They replied, "That's the way it is, that's the way it has always been, that's the way it always will be. There's nothing anyone can do about it, so just accept it."

Things weren't always the best in Chicago, but Chicago certainly looked better than down south in Macon, Tennessee. I was forced to live in two different worlds, and each year as I grew older and recognized the differences between them, it got tougher and tougher to spend my summers down south.

The two worlds were on a collision path with each other, and it was only a matter of time until they collided. The collision happened during the summer of my junior year in high school; that was the final year I ever went down south. I drove separately that summer as I had passed my driver's test and had my own car — a beat-up old hooptie. That would be the last time I would see my grandparents in Tennessee.

I'd driven all day and finally arrived in Macon and decided it was best if I gassed up in town before I headed out to the farm. I pulled up to the gas pump in front of the general store, which wasn't really a gas station — just a gas pump that was outside the store. I got out and began to pump gas in my car.

The owner of the general store came out and said, "Is that your car, boy?"

Tennessee Summers cont'd

I wasn't in the mood for "that" kind of talk. To be perfectly honest, I shouldn't even have been there in the first place. My fuse was growing shorter with every summer I spent down south, but I knew my mom really wanted me to come down one more year and visit with my grandparents and get away from the city for a while.

I looked up at the owner, stared him straight in the eye, and said, "Who are you calling 'boy'?"

He replied, "Mind your manners now, boy, you mind your manners."

"I'm not your boy. There's a man standing here in front of you, and you need to recognize that."

I took the pump out of my gas tank, placed it back in the holder, put the money on top of the pump, and walked away. He grabbed the money and stomped back into his general store. I drove the seven miles to my grandfather's farm, fuming at what had happened. I told my grandfather what had occurred in town and he said, "You best leave right now, Grandson. Leave right now and don't ever come back."

I gave both my grandmother and grandfather a big hug and drove out of that town. I've never returned to Macon, Tennessee, and I don't plan on going there anytime soon. I don't think I'll ever go back.

A couple of years later before my grandfather passed, when he and my grandmother were in Chicago to visit my mom and say goodbye to me before I left to go to basic training, we had a discussion about that particular day. My grandfather told me that later on that same evening a truck with a bunch of white men in the back carrying rifles came out to the farm looking for me. My grandfather told them that I had gone back up north. Their comment to my grandfather was, "He best stay up there. No good will come if he ever comes back."

I never understood why my grandfather and grandmother allowed themselves to be shamed, disrespected, and ridiculed. Years later as an adult when I reflected back on those summers, I had a feeling they allowed it because they thought they were the minority down south, and

The Stump

that was just the way things were. They didn't think they had a choice for it to be any different. They accepted it and considered it their way of life. They thought they didn't dare go against the norm for fear they might find themselves, as African Americans, hanging from a tree, or shot when they were alone.

Their generation had grown up, heard, and saw the prejudice firsthand. It was a time during our American history down south where many police and white men seemed to be on the same page when it came to the law — or lack of enforcing the law in terms of black equality. As a small boy who spent his summers down south on a farm, I personally had heard white men comment that they could shoot and kill a "N" and there wouldn't be a court in the state that would convict him. That was my grandparents' reality, their way of life, but it certainly wasn't going to be mine.

My grandfather had fought for his country; had served with honor and dignity. He, however, came back to a country that didn't give him the respect he had so rightly earned and deserved. He returned home and found he was a nothing and a nobody; he was just another "N". I couldn't accept that, nor could I tolerate to be in his world. I knew I wouldn't survive if I stayed in Tennessee. I was taught to be a proud black man who was responsible to fight for what he believed in, to look a man in the eye and never back down.

A conflict constantly raged inside of me during those summers I spent in the South. I kept it at bay, dormant, because I was not in a position or had the knowledge to make a decision that could change what I was going through. My mom knew it was just a matter of time before the trips down south would end for me once I got old enough and started thinking for myself.

I do give all honor and praise to the Almighty for giving my grandparents the will to persevere. They endured much and received so little. When I look at the world today, I wonder how they would react to the

Tennessee Summers cont'd

time that I live in. I think they would find inner pride and hold their heads up, proud that we have made such great strides in equality. Not to say we don't have many miles to go yet, and not to say that blacks still don't face many problems yet today. However, the changes that have occurred over the years has made it so much better than what they experienced during the time they lived. Deep down I'm sure they dreamed and wanted better, yet never thought equality would ever come. They stayed completely silent; I, of course, could not.

My grandparents never complained about anything. They were hard workers and did what they had to do to survive. I think my grandparents were like any other African Americans that lived in the South during that time. I think they wanted a better life. They wanted change. But I think they believed in something much deeper that kept them going and promised rewards in the end.

My grandmother was very religious, as was my grandfather. I think their faith helped them weather through a lot of the difficulties they faced each and every day. They kept their faith through all of their trials, and in the end, they believed their reward would be with the Almighty Himself. All their suffering here on Earth would be carried away. My grandparents are long passed on, but one thing I do know: They are both sitting on the right hand of the Almighty looking down at me and smiling.

Grandma and Grandpa. (Author collection)

Chapter 9

MOVING OBJECTS

My uncles (from my mom's side) were known for driving fast cars. Not just around the city of Chicago, but from Chicago to Memphis. They called it the US Highway 1 Run. As a little kid I didn't know what all of that meant. All I knew was when I heard those loud engines, I knew the Fords and my uncles were close at hand. Their cars had the biggest engines that could fit under the hood, and I remember all of them were painted jet black.

One summer my uncles talked with my mom and said, "It's time for Terry to start being a man. Let us take him on a run." I had no clue what any of that meant. All I knew was I was nine years old and my uncles said that was old enough to go with them and be a man. I was up for the task.

My mom said yes I could go, so I quickly climbed in the front seat with my favorite uncle before she had a chance to change her mind. I had to sit up real straight because if I slouched I couldn't see over the dashboard. I wanted to make sure I didn't miss anything. There weren't any seat belts, or else they were tucked down beneath the seats, so I didn't worry about buckling up. Nobody said I had to wear one, so I was set to go.

The Stump

My uncle climbed in and sat behind the wheel with a big smile on his face. He said, "Are you ready to be a man?"

I answered, "Yes, sir. Let's do this!"

He started the engine, tapped the gas pedal, revved up the engine, put the car in gear, and stepped on the gas. It was like we were shot out of a cannon. My uncles used to say, "Hit it and get it." I didn't understand that phrase until my uncle hit the gas and he certainly got all the engine had to offer. I was thrown back into my seat, and that kind of got me thinking I wished I had a seat belt to put on, but off we went.

We completed the Chicago to Memphis run well under eight hours, which was pretty good time for a six hundred-mile drive when the speed limit was still fifty-five. My maiden voyage was on an early Saturday morning, and by Saturday afternoon we all were in Memphis and had pulled into an old farmhouse I wasn't familiar with. It wasn't my grandparents' farm, but I recognized some of the men, as I had seen them when we butchered pigs in the summer.

Each of my uncles went around to the back of their cars and opened up their trunks. I went with my favorite uncle whom I rode with to open up our trunk and looked inside. To me it looked like any other normal trunk, but as he ran his hand along the inside of the trunk, I heard something snap, and a little compartment opened. He lifted out what appeared to be bottles of water and gave them to the men who were at the farm.

We stayed for supper and then got back on the road and headed home. It was an uneventful trip. I thought if this was part of being a man, that wasn't too bad; I could handle it. As I got older I figured out they were running moonshine, making it in Chicago and running it down to Memphis. They said I brought them good luck that day!

Late one evening after one of the runs, when I was in the car with my dad on my way back from Memphis, I heard loud sirens, and when

Moving Objects

I looked out the back window I saw flashing lights. It was a highway patrolman. My dad slowed down, pulled the car over to the side of the highway, and put the car in park. I saw the patrolman approach from the driver's side of the car. My father looked at me and said, "It's going to be okay, Son, don't worry. I wasn't speeding. I was taking my time. I'm not sure why he pulled us over."

As my father rolled down the window, the highway patrolman shined his flashlight in my father's face, and then moved the light and shined it on my face before he moved it back to my father's.

The patrolman said, "Is this your car, boy?"

My father responded, "Yes, officer, this is my car. I would appreciate it if you would not use those choice of words around my son."

"Boy, I'll use any kind of words I want. License and registration."

My father produced his license and registration and said, "Can you tell me what the problem is, officer?"

"You just sit there and wait, boy. I will tell you what the problem is when I'm good and ready to."

"Officer, what is your problem? This is a man sitting here in front of you and you had better well acknowledge that."

"Boy, get out of the car!"

My father turned to me and said, "Son, don't move. I'll be right back."

It seemed like forever, an eternity, but perhaps was only a few minutes until my dad returned. My father said, "Are you ready to go, Son?"

I don't know what took place between my father and that officer that evening. What I do know is my dad returned and we rode on home. We never spoke about that ride home ever, and when I thought about it later, I decided I didn't want to know what took place that evening. We didn't talk about it to anyone, not even my mom.

Later on that same year my father purchased bikes for all of us kids to learn how to ride. My father wouldn't allow us to ride our bikes on

The Stump

the front sidewalks or on the street, so we rode them in the alleyways in the back of the houses where the entrance to the garages were located. After a couple of weeks of riding with training wheels on, my younger brother and I got the hang of it and rode solo.

My older sister was a little slower to learn how to ride her bike, even with the training wheels on, but one morning my sister got it in her head she was going to take the training wheels off and ride without them. She started at one end of the alley and was determined to make it to the opposite end without falling off her bike. When she started out in those first beginning seconds, it looked like she was going to do just that, but somehow my sister couldn't quite get the steering down and off she went, headed straight for the closest garage door. She bounced off that first one and headed for the next door. I guess that was how she intended to make her way down the alley, using the pinball approach.

She was well on her way to hitting every last one of the garage doors in our back alley when my brother and I decided we didn't want to be around to see how her trip ended up; we ran back to our house. As we came through the door I heard my father yell at my mom, "Alrine, I got the neighbors calling me. Now you go get that daughter of ours because she is tearing up every garage with that bike of hers."

Mom replied, "She's going to be all right. She's just learning how to ride. Maybe we should take her to the park; there's less things to hit there."

My dad said, "I don't think that would help. I don't think she'll ever learn how to ride that bike. You two go back outside and get your sister."

We both responded, "Yes, sir."

My brother and I went back outside and hauled our sister kicking and screaming off her bike as she was down toward the end of the alley. We did manage so save the last few remaining garage doors that she hadn't gotten to yet. My sister tried a few more times to ride in the park, but without any side bumpers to keep her steering straight, she just couldn't get it. To this day my sister still can't ride a bike. Some things are just *not* meant to be.

As we got older my mom decided she was going to take all of us out for a driving lesson. She took us to a big parking lot early one Saturday morning before any cars were out and about. She instructed us on various maneuvers — straight and parallel parking, the three-point turn — and finished up with how to back up.

I drove first and practiced those things my mom had instructed us on. Then my younger brother and I switched positions and he did the same. We had no problems. Next up was my sister. This would be the same one who never learned how to ride the bike! She was all smiles, excited it was finally her time to practice. As she got out of the car and climbed behind the wheel on the driver's side, my brother and I both jumped out of the car, ran, and stood on the curb.

My mom looked at both of us and said, "Now you two know you are being mean to your sister."

I replied, "No, Mom, we just want to live."

My sister said, "You are being mean."

My bother replied, "We love you, Sis, but we're not getting back in the car. You're on your own."

My sister never got a driver's license either. Guess she and moving objects just don't get along.

My mother always had a great love for Cadillacs, and that was the car I learned how to drive on. She used to tell me I had the foot of my father and her driving talent. Besides taking me to the big empty parking lot to drive around and practice on, my mom wanted to make sure I was good enough to drive anywhere in the world. There was a busy street close to where I lived named St. Lawrence. It was a two-way street with cars parked on both sides. Now you can imagine what that felt like just learning how to drive and my mom making me practice on one of the busiest streets that I knew of. Not only was it busy, it was

The Stump

narrow because cars were parked on both sides of the street. To top it all off, I was driving her 1968 Cadillac de Ville, a beast of a car — big, long, and wide.

My mom told me, "If you can drive St. Lawrence in my Cadillac, there's no street in the world you can't drive on, and I know you are ready for your driver's license."

My fear as I headed out on my maiden voyage to St. Lawrence was I knew I had to steer clear of those parked cars and yet stay away from the cars coming directly at me. I also knew St. Lawrence wasn't a particularly wide street by any means, and I was driving a huge Cadillac.

I got to the red stoplight, where I would turn onto St. Lawrence. As I waited for that light to turn green so I could turn, I said a prayer to the Almighty above. "Please help me get to the other end and let me do better than Sis did on her bike. I promise I'll be nicer to her if you help me out."

I'm not sure how much was luck that day, how much was skill, and how much was the Lord's doing, but I did manage to drive down St. Lawrence without hitting anything. Mom took me several more times up and down that street on different occasions until I got comfortable with the Cadillac. We finally decided it was time for me to take my driver's test.

You just gotta love best-laid plans. Five days before I was due to take my driver's test my mom put her car, the Cadillac, in the shop for maintenance work to ensure it was okay for me to take my test on. The day of my driver's test arrived and the shop called my mom and told her the car would not be ready. I was without wheels.

My mom talked to her brother, and my uncle agreed to let me use one of their cars to test with. He had a Firebird that was much smaller than the Cadillac and it all sounded good in theory, but I was not used to driving that car. I was not comfortable driving it at all.

"I'm not sure about this, Mom," I said. "I've never driven a Firebird."

Both my uncle and my mom said, "You're going to be all right. You'll do just fine."

I don't have to tell you what the outcome of that was. I didn't pass my driver's test that day. I didn't know where any of the controls were located, and I had never practiced parallel parking with that car. The whole experience was a nightmare.

A few weeks later I returned to the DMV with the Cadillac that was now fixed. To my surprise I got the same driving instructor I had before.

He said, "You back again? You didn't fair out too well last time, and I see you have something much bigger than you drove before. You sure someone like you can handle a car that big?"

I looked at him and thought, *I'm going to show you and everybody else what I can do, because there isn't nothing I can't do with this Cadillac.*

You guessed it. I did get my driver's license that day.

The instructor looked at me after we were done and said, "I guess you showed everybody today including me, didn't you?"

I looked at him and smiled, driver's license in hand.

Chapter 10

A TOUCH OF GOD'S HANDS

During high school I helped out doing janitorial support at the brick three-story apartment building we lived in. One of my duties was to dump the garbage cans that sat out on everyone's stair landing into the one large dumpster for the apartment building. Each landing had a big aluminum trash can with a lid on it. As fate would have it, they happened to be the same type of garbage cans the Bear would bang on each morning to wake us up during basic training. Maybe it was better I didn't know that at the time!

I grabbed the second floor can and brought it downstairs and emptied it in the larger dumpster the garbage men would empty. As I walked up the stairs to the third floor landing, I noticed the steps were weather beaten, dry rotted, wobbly, and in need of repair. An eerie feeling crept over me.

I arrived at the third floor landing and made a mental note to tell the maintenance man to check out these stairs. As I lifted the trash can up, I again had a strong feeling that something wasn't right.

The Stump

I turned to make my way downstairs with the trash can in hand but when I took my first step, the entire stairwell fell away; it folded up like an accordion, disappearing right out from under me. I dropped the trash can and the lid went flying as I tried to grab the railing, but I only found air. In seconds the ground came up fast and my back hit hard — I felt a sharp pain. The collapsed staircase made a deafening sound that brought my mom running outside. She screamed and hollered out my name. She rushed me to the University of Chicago Medical Center and the doctors immediately rushed me in, took x-rays, and then admitted me to a room.

I lay in the hospital bed and listened to a bunch of doctors who hovered outside my room. One said, "That's not possible."

I wanted someone to come in and talk to me so I knew what was going on. When the doctors did enter my room they stood by my bed, looked at me, and then left to find my mom.

My mom came back alone and said, "You're going to be okay, but they want to keep you overnight."

I said, "I feel fine. Why can't I go home?"

"They want you to stay here for the night."

"Somebody needs to tell me what's going on!"

A doctor must have heard my raised voice. He came in, stood with my mom, and said, "What happened to you we can't explain."

I exclaimed, "What are you talking about?"

The doctor continued, "There was an incident on the North Side today very similar to what happened to you, except you were on a higher floor. That young man broke his arm, fractured his back, and he is currently in the ICU. Even though you were up on a higher floor, all we can find on you is a cut on your back, some bruising, and that's about it." He shook his head. "That's not possible."

"What do you mean that's not possible?" I asked.

"The force you took from hitting the ground from a three-story fall should have put you in a body cast at a minimum. You are lucky to be alive."

"What?" I hadn't realized the seriousness of my accident.

"We need to keep you here for observations and make sure there are not any internal injuries."

"I feel fine."

"You're staying here. No arguing about that."

I did stay in the hospital as the doctor ordered. They wouldn't let me go anywhere, wouldn't let me eat, and even put an IV in me. At least whatever fluids they gave me took my appetite away. I stayed there until noon the next day until I was finally released.

Several doctors checked in on me throughout the morning. A nurse came in with the last doctor, who gave the final nod and said, "Okay, we think you are ready to go home."

I said, "I know I'm definitely ready to go home."

I jumped out of bed and the doctor said, "You really are special."

I replied, "No, Doc, I'm just an ordinary guy."

"No, you are very special. There's something about you. I can't put my hands on it, but what happened to you in this hospital, we call that a miracle. That was truly miraculous that you walked away from that fall almost without a scratch. You need to really think about that."

I looked at him and walked off. The University Hospital was only five or six blocks from where we lived, so I jogged slowly all the way home. I felt a little stiff from lying in the hospital bed for a day, and it felt good to stretch and get my muscles loosened up.

Once home I got cleaned up and rested a bit until my mom got home from work. That evening I sat and talked with her. She knew I was going to be released but didn't know when. She had asked the doctors

The Stump

if I would need a ride home from the hospital, but they told her I'd be fine and could make my way home by myself.

My mom said, "You have been touched by God. I talked with your grandmother about what happened and she said it's time for you to be reborn again."

I remembered being reborn when I was a little boy that summer down south when my top got stuck on the roof. My grandma helped me out and got the Almighty himself to touch me that day in the church. My mom discussed it with our pastor, and later on that month he re-baptized me. One would think I'd be good to go with all the baptizing and reborn again moments I've had; maybe that helped keep me safe when those stairs collapsed. What I didn't know was I would have one more baptism left to do — that would be for my soul mate!

Over the years, I do think there has been a special hand that has followed me around and steered me safely throughout my life. There have been many situations over the years that I've come out of missions without a scratch, when in all reality I should be ten feet under. In my thirty-seven plus years of serving in the military, I've had more than my share of events that have gone wrong. Intel that was way off that put my team in a world of hurt — those times especially I shouldn't have come home ... but there it is.

It took me a while to reflect upon what had happened the day the apartment stairs collapsed. It didn't register until much later after I got out of the hospital what the doctor tried to get me to understand. When I compared my accident to the other kid, he was carried off in an ambulance with sustained injuries that included a broken back. I was higher up than he was when the entire stairway gave way and I hit with such force and unbelievable impact that it threw me back up and bounced me back down. I didn't have a cushioned jacket to help soften the impact either; I only had an ordinary thin T-shirt on. To walk away with a small cut on my back, that's more than just a miracle. That is God's hand and His guiding grace that helped me walk away from that one.

Mom and me. (Author collection)

Chapter 11

THE BASEBALL GAME

Summers spent down south were not always about hard work. After church on Sundays, after farm chores were done, we usually had some spare time to play. We fished, swam in the creek, rode the big plow horses, and tossed our tops around. But every once in a while on a Saturday afternoon if we had finished working in the fields, we headed out to see a baseball game.

My grandfather, uncles, and I piled into grandpa's farm truck and drove to see other black men play baseball. Back in my Grandpa's day, the Negro Leagues were very popular. My grandpa said he and some of my uncles even played ball in the leagues. I don't doubt it. They sure taught me how to play, and they told me plenty of stories, ones I'm sure Grandmother didn't know about.

Before 1947, the year when Jackie Robinson broke the color barrier, blacks were not allowed to play ball in the major leagues. It's sad to think that playing our national pastime at its highest level was reserved for only whites.

As far back as the 1880s, African Americans had formed their own non-professional teams. By the 1920s, the Negro Leagues were professionally run organizations. By the late '50s and '60s, most talented African American ball players had entered the major and minor

The Stump

leagues, and eventually the Negro Leagues ceased to exist.* I caught the tail end of the last Negro games played. Those were some of my fondest memories I had down south, and I sure did learn a lot about playing the game.

I played baseball all four years in high school and was a pitcher, a southpaw. At the time when I went to high school on the South Side, all the high schools we played against were predominately black. It wasn't because Chicago wasn't integrated at the time. The geographical placement of the high schools in the city lent itself to whites going to all-white schools, and they played other white schools. I had never played against a white team. I don't even remember being on the same field as a white player. The only time you would have had a chance to play against a white team was if we got in the playoffs. That chance came my way my senior year.

I had a pretty good senior year pitching, and our team had a darn good year playing ball — so good, in fact, that we found ourselves in the playoffs. My grandfather happened to be in the city that year visiting my mom, shortly before he passed, and was there for the playoff game. Our coach told us we were going to play an all-white team, and I was told I was going to be the starting pitcher.

I wasn't sure how I was going to pitch against a white player or how I felt about that. I had never pitched to a white kid before. I hadn't figured out that a white player was no different than me, that he was just another player. My psyche got the best of me.

I think my grandfather saw fear in my eyes the day of the game. Before I walked out on the field, he came into the locker room to talk to me and said, "How are you feeling, Grandson? You ready?"

I looked at my grandfather, and I know he saw I was more than a little scared. I decided the best option was to be honest. I hesitated before I said, "I'm not sure about this, Grandpa."

The Baseball Game

"Grandson, I want you to listen to me. You own the plate, and there is a man standing at the plate. So you have to make sure to do everything you can to get him off the plate."

"How do I do that, Grandfather?"

"This is what I want you to do. Throw your fastest pitch to the inside, close and tight. If that batter moves and takes a step back off the plate, Grandson, you own him."

Being a smart aleck, I said, "What if he don't move? What do I do then?"

My grandfather took both of his hands, placed them on my shoulders, and brazenly said, "Oh trust me, he will move!"

As my grandfather placed his hands on my shoulders and spoke, I was taken back to the Stump and I heard Mrs. Hannaberry preach, *"Do you believe? You have to believe in yourself, Terry."*

As my grandfather tightened his grip on my shoulders, bringing me back to the present, he said, "Do you believe? Do you believe, Grandson?"

Resolved and resolute, I replied, "Yes, I do, Grandfather."

He ended with, "Good. Now go show me."

I stood on the mound and looked down the pipe. During those Tennessee summers my grandfather and uncles had taught me about the all-important "tunnel." Block everything out — everything to your left, everything to your right, every person in the stands. Just look down the tunnel. See nothing; hear nothing. Nothing exists but the pipe.

I could, however, hear my heart thumping like it was going to come out of my chest. No one had told me how to keep that quiet. The batter crowded the plate, tight and right on top of it. I went into my windup and ripped it as hard as I could, a fastball to the inside. The batter rocked and took two steps back.

The Stump

I was so relieved. I looked over in the stands at my grandfather, and I could see the joy and smile he had on his face — how proud he was. I told myself I'm going to win this game for him today. And I did. I felt there was nothing I couldn't accomplish. I knew I had him, that first batter, and every last one of 'em!

Chapter 12

HANGING OUT

I'VE ALWAYS BEEN A STRONG-WILLED PERSON. I account that largely to my upbringing from my father and grandfather. My father used to say, "Pay your own way, go your own way, and stand up for what you believe in."

My grandfather used to say, "It's not their decision. It's not our decision. It is your decision. Only you can make it for yourself."

During high school I hung out with my partners and we were in the habit of cutting class. My partners cut their regular classes. I, on the other hand, only cut study hall. I stood around with them outside the school, talked trash, laughed, and joked around. All the while I had my ear tuned to the bell to listen for it to ring. The first bell meant I needed to move out and head back into school; by that second bell I needed to be in my seat or else I would be late.

I made sure I only cut study hall and made time to get my studying done so I kept my grades up. My partners thought I was just like them and skipped classes, but I didn't want to be like them. Regardless of their faults, they still were good guys and were my partners, but I definitely wasn't going to be standing around in Chicago after we graduated. I was getting out of here. I suppose people like Mr. Dittle never thought we

The Stump

were going to make anything out of ourselves, but I was determined I was going to prove him and others like him wrong.

Sometimes I hung out with my partners on weekends too, but anytime a group of blacks walked the streets together the police would view us as troublemakers, regardless of what we were or were not doing. In my neighborhood if you hung out on a street corner that was a sure way to attract the attention of the cops. They would pull up in their police car and get out with billy clubs already in hand — their other one close to their pistol ready to draw on you.

They would say, "We know what this is and you know what to do. Assume the position."

My partners knew exactly what to do. They stood spread eagle against the nearest building, feet and hands spread. All the while the police waited for them to make a wrong move and looked for an opportunity or excuse to use their clubs.

When my partners used to say, "Let's go hang out on the corner," I would reply, "What is wrong with you guys? You know that just means trouble. Why go looking for it? Every time we go up near that corner trouble is going to find us as sure as we are standing there."

I guess they could never think of anything else they would rather do, and it didn't take them long before they were standing on the corner talking their usual trash talk. I, on the other hand, walked off and went in the opposite direction. I would look back and sure enough, I could see them in the distance, assuming the position with cops all around them. I continued walking, shook my head, and thought, *When are you ever going to learn*?

During the four years I hung out with my partners in high school, I made many good memories with them, but at the end of the day it was sad. They never graduated from high school and I would bet they never got their GEDs either.

Mrs. Hannaberry's influence guided those in my neighborhood. However, we did not all attend the same high school. Some went to the Catholic high school. I used my aunt's address and went to what my parents felt was a better high school than our local one. We continued to make time to meet back at the Stump, where we talked about our different high school experiences with Mrs. Hannaberry.

Unfortunately, my partners I hung out with at my high school did not live in my neighborhood and were not exposed to Mrs. Hannaberry's positive influence. Perhaps if they had, their lives might have turned out differently.

At the end of my senior year one of my partners said, "Hey, man, I saw your name on the graduation list. What's up with that? The rest of us aren't graduating."

I replied, "Oh really. Looks like someone must have made a mistake."

"I don't know. You're the only Terry Braddock in the whole school."

"Yeah, think you're right; guess I must be graduating then." I walked off with a smile on my face and thought, *Momma didn't raise no fool here.* Back over my shoulder I replied, "I'll catch you later."

Not only did I graduate from Hirsch High in 1973, that was also the year our basketball team took city and state championships.* We were always regarded as a good Chicago high school basketball team with the possibility of taking city, but no one ever thought we could compete at state level with some of the top Illinois high schools that were playing in the state that year. Once it was announced we were on our way to state, we were not ranked favorably to do well.

Hirsch High School was an all-black high school playing in the state tournament against all-white basketball teams that were highly ranked and regarded as having the best players in Illinois. Racial views still lingered that black athletes lacked the same mental capacity as whites to play ball at such a high level.† What they didn't know was we had players who would eventually go on to play professional basketball in the NBA.

The Stump

Hirsch High School. (Author collection)

Our number one player was Ricky Green, who led the team in scoring and was also the team captain. He would later be drafted out of college by the Golden State Warriors and play many years in the NBA.

We took spectator buses down to Champaign to cheer our team on, and we shocked the entire state of Illinois when we took it all that year. The tournament director hated to give Hirsch High the trophy. It almost brought him to tears to have to present it to our team and not to one of the other schools.

Our basketball team's state championship made Mayor Richard J. Daley of Chicago proud. He and the entire city was so honored with our basketball team's accomplishment they gave our high school a parade and also gave us the privilege to graduate from one of the most visible places in Chicago at that time: McCormick Place. History was written that year, and all of us seniors would always have the opportunity to say we attended Hirsch High School and graduated in 1973 when our class was labeled as city and state champions.

Those four years I hung out with my partners I was well aware of my choice to skip class. I, however, made the conscious decision to ensure I only missed study hall. I made the choice to study and ensure I kept my grades up so I could graduate. Those choices I made back then certainly had an impact on the life I lead today. I would not be where I am now had I made the decisions my partners did. Their decision to skip school and not graduate was a direct link for them to remain in the ghetto. For me that was not an option I was going to entertain.

I have always believed we are controllers of our destiny. To me it's simple: If no one has a gun held to your head or a knife put to your throat then you have total control over decisions you make in your life. There is a quote from the movie *Renaissance Man*, when Danny DeVito in the role of Bill Rago says, "... the choices you make dictate the life you lead."* I believe those words even to this day.

Mrs. Hannaberry always had a way of keeping us on our toes, and she liked to keep us thinking. One day at the Stump she said, *"There's a big ocean out there, and although you might think there is nothing in it because from the surface it just looks like plain empty water, oh that is when you are going to have a real big surprise. That ocean is filled with many different wonders, and all you have to do..."* She paused and made sure we all listened to her. *"All you have to do is just let yourself experience it. And I can promise you this, you will never be disappointed."*

I knew Mrs. Hannaberry was right. Although I had already experienced lots of different things living in the ghetto and spending summers down south, I knew there was still a lot in that ocean I had not yet experienced, and I couldn't wait to get out there and see what was hiding underneath. I had already enlisted in the delayed entry program and joined the United States Army. That would provide a huge ocean for me to explore and experience. I was one step closer to getting out. I was determined — to make it out, and stay out!

Chapter 13

THEY CAME BACK

Mrs. Hannaberry tried her best to keep us away from the gangs so we didn't get caught up in gang activity. She kept a very close watch on us; asked where we were going, what we were doing, who we were hanging with. She was on us constantly and did a good job of keeping us on the straight and narrow. One thing about Mrs. Hannaberry, this white woman didn't play. She wasn't mean; she just demanded respect for ourselves as well as for herself.

She said, *"Don't play me, don't lie to me, and don't mess around with me. Always tell me the truth. No matter how hard it is, just tell me the truth."* That's the way she rolled.

As we got older and headed into our teenage years, she couldn't help herself and tried to play matchmaker. I wasn't going for any of that! Those were the best times for me growing up as a kid on the South Side. I cherished each day I spent on the Stump. It didn't matter what time I left the house in the morning; I knew I would end up at the Stump by the end of my day, sometimes talking into the wee hours of the night.

Mrs. Hannaberry told me, *"Terry, I expect better of you. I know you have it inside you. Look at me. I'm never wrong — remember that."*

The Stump

I replied, "Yes, ma'am."

During one of my military leaves I earned from the Army, I went back home and walked over to the Stump to see if Mrs. Hannaberry was still there. She was, although I noticed she had really started to age. I had never thought about how old Mrs. Hannaberry might be. She said, *"See, I always knew you were one of my special ones."* That was the last time I would see and talk with her.

The inner city of Chicago was no different than any other big city. As I grew up I developed friendships with other young boys growing up in the neighborhood. I had a handful of close friends — David, Carl, Tony, and Albert — and of course my little brother Junior tagged along with us. We went everywhere together. As a matter of fact we formed our own neighborhood watch club. In a sense we looked like a little gang ourselves, but didn't want to be referred to as a gang so we called ourselves "The Sixty-First Street Boys." We even got black baseball caps with the numbers "61st" on the front and the word "Boys" on the back.

For some strange reason I seemed to be the leader of the club. I didn't ask to be; that was just the way it was. We had club meetings, club dues, a treasurer, and secretary (my influence from the Cub Scouts). We were high speed and even formed our own softball, basketball, and touch football teams, but most importantly we formed a neighborhood watch.

Our primary duty was to look out for the older people in our neighborhood, but we also watched out for the little kids who played in the streets and in their yards. Neighbors would let us know if we needed to pick up groceries for someone if they weren't feeling well or needed help carrying their groceries home. Many others needed help cutting their lawns. We always made it a point to make sure they knew we were there to help.

Mr. Parker owned the local corner newsstand. It was just a little shack; had a little table and a door so he could lock his stuff up at night.

He sold newspapers, magazines, chewing gum, and candy bars. He was up in age, having served in WWI and WWII. We considered him to be the last of the dinosaurs, but he treated us well and liked to tell us his war stories. No one messed with Mr. Parker because us Sixty-First Street Boys always looked out for him.

We tried to make time during the day to drop in and check on him now and then, and assured him we'd be back to walk him home when he closed his stand at night. We didn't want Mr. Parker to get robbed or mugged. If Mr. Parker needed to stop off at the grocery store before he went home, we were always there to help carry his groceries.

On one Saturday evening, David, Tony, and I walked Mr. Parker home. As we approached his front porch he said, "Why don't you boys have a seat here and talk to me a little bit."

David replied, "So what's up, Mr. Parker? You got some things going on you want to talk to us about?"

Mr. Parker replied, "I want to talk to you three about what's been happening in our neighborhood."

I replied, "Yeah, Mr. Parker, there's a lot been going on the last couple of months."

He continued, "Guys, I want you to know I was in this neighborhood long before you were born. I have watched this neighborhood grow and change, but you want to know something? I still believe in this neighborhood and I still believe in the people. I trust my fellow neighbors, but most of all, I trust you."

Tony replied, "We really appreciate that, Mr. Parker. It's because of people like you that we like to look out for everyone."

I said, "Mr. Parker, things are going to get better. Just you wait and see."

Mr. Parker said, "You young men know that I still believe in this neighborhood and I believe that you will do something to protect our rights. Now head out, boys, and have a good night."

The Stump

"You too, Mr. Parker," we all said as we got up and left.

I looked at Tony and David and said, "Let's go talk."

Later that evening the Sixty-First Street Boys came together in my basement, which we called the clubhouse. I said, "Listen up, guys. Reason why I asked you all to come together and called this late meeting is because we just came from walking Mr. Parker home. He was telling us he believes in the neighborhood but is concerned with what's been happening lately. Now I know we all have seen activity going on in the hood. I think it's time to do something about it."

David said, "I'm all in, but we need to make sure whatever we do we do it right."

Tony piped up, "Whatever we do we need to be aware we might be starting something we might not be able to finish. Have you forgot there's more of them than there is of us?"

Alvin added, "You guys know what I'm all about. I'm not looking for trouble, but if trouble finds me I'm ready for it. All I'm saying is, are we looking for trouble?"

I spoke to the group. "I think we all need to understand something. Trouble is already here, and I don't see it going anywhere anytime soon. It's spreading like a cancer. If the Sixty-First Boys don't cut it out, it's going to affect everything in the hood."

David said, "What do you suggest we do?"

"First things first, guys. Let's get the neighborhood together on this. I want you to knock on every door; I want you to talk to everybody. We need the entire neighborhood in on the watch, not just the Sixty-First Street Boys. We have to get everyone involved. If you see something, say something. If you hear something, report it. I see it this way: If all of us, and I mean everybody in the neighborhood, if we all come together, then nothing can stop us.

"I never expected the Sixty-First Boys to go into this alone, but I do think everyone in the hood feels just like we do. They just aren't saying anything. So why don't we become their voice and say what they are afraid to say? Not now, not here, and definitely not in my hood, the bucks stop here. All in favor say 'aye'; all opposed say 'nay.' . . . Motion carried; the ayes have it. Let's get it done."

It was a sight to see how the entire neighborhood came together. The Sixty-First Street Boys knocked on doors and talked to all the neighbors. Some of the adults even contacted the cops, and to our surprise they worked with us to crack down on the violence. We changed what was happening on our streets in our neighborhood we considered home. The gang activity slowed, and within a couple of months it was pretty much completely gone. It never came back during the time the Sixty-First Street Boys were around.

Mr. Parker talked to us boys many months after the neighborhood was cleaned up and told us, "The gift of service. I'm proud of you boys. You guys did your part, and even when it got tough you held the course and didn't give up. You were part of something that was bigger than yourself. Remember John F. Kennedy's words: 'Ask not what your country can do for you — ask what you can do for your country.'* Kennedy was talking to all of us. I, like many others, felt he was talking directly to me. America didn't owe me; I owed America. I myself have given. I have served. I have done my part and more. I was part of something bigger than myself, and now so have you."

There was a set of kids who were a couple of years or more ahead of me in school. You would think they would have been our mentors and would have wanted to set a good example for us to follow behind them. Unfortunately we weren't so lucky to have that available to us in our neighborhood. The older kids dressed real nice, had new cars and flashy girlfriends, wore gold chains, and never were without a pocketful of money. It didn't take a lot of common sense to know where it all came from. The one thing we always saw was the police constantly stopping them, all the time.

The Stump

My friends and I sat and talked amongst ourselves, not only at the Stump, but other places in the neighborhood as well — the park mostly because we played a lot of ball there. We talked about what not to do when it came down to those older boys. There were many times when they came at us trying to get us to join their way of life. We could count on Mrs. Hannaberry at the Stump to keep us straight. She was our voice of reason. She talked common sense. But most of all she was just there — there for us when we needed her to be.

I said to Mrs. Hannaberry one day, *"You are a straight shooter. You always tell it like it is and you always talk from the heart."*

She replied, *"I will never lie to you. I will never shortchange you. I will always speak the truth to you whether you like it or not. I expect the same out of you."*

Three of those older young men in our neighborhood who talked to us were named Big George, Laponds, and Cossie. These three individuals lived the life of flash and fast action. They were always in and out of jail and constantly had run-ins with the cops.

Big George found himself in front of a judge, who told him, "You only have two options: go to jail or join the Army."

Big George joined the Army. Yeah, you guessed it, Big George's time with Uncle Sam didn't last too long. He got chaptered out of the Army for drug use. One Saturday morning I came down the street and happened to look up at the corner building, where I saw Big George standing on the third floor landing.

Big George always called me Little Man, and as I walked closer and we caught each other's eye, he said, "What's up, Little Man?"

I replied, "Nothing much. What's up with you? I thought you was doing your thing in the Army?"

"Nah, the Army ain't for me, man. Army ain't no place for a black man. The white man has us right where he wants us. You listen to me, Little Man: You don't want to be a black man in a white man's army, because you're not a soldier — you're just another "N" wearing a soldier's uniform. Now you need to listen to me, Little Man, 'cause I've been there, I know firsthand what's going on. Do you understand what I'm saying to you?"

"Big George, I hear you, but I'm going to make up my own mind and go my own way. Believe this, anything I want I'm not afraid to go after it, and I'm sure not afraid to earn it."

"All right, Little Man, you got a reputation around this neighborhood for going your own way and not listening to nobody. But you mark my words, when it's your turn and if you do decide to go in the white man's army, you're going to come back too. You see, Little Man, we all come back, right back here. Where else do we have to go?"

"Big George, that's bull. Anywhere is better than here. I'm not coming back. When I leave I'm gone for good, you can believe that."

"All right, Little Man. All right."

Days after that conversation with Big George, I heard he was in trouble with the cops again and got locked up. I never saw him after that. Laponds and Cossie continued to try and push us boys into the life of drugs and crime, dangling the spoils of that life in front of us. I never understood why they didn't realize life expectancy in that world was probably no more than twenty-one years old. If you made it to twenty-five you were doing real good. In the end I guess they did know that, but they never thought they would get out of their twenties so what did it matter? They lived their lives fast, knowing their days were numbered.

Every now and then when I went back and visited during those earlier years on leave from the Army, most of the guys I grew up with to include some of the Sixty-First Street Boys were either in jail or had been killed. They came back. I never did; at least not to stay. If Kathleen and I go back to visit my family, two days at the most, my PTSD creeps in around the edges. Time to get out of the city.

Chapter 14

THE SIXTH SENSE

My mom told me at a young age, "You are very special." I suppose all moms tell their children this. My mom perhaps meant it in a different way than most. She would tell me, "Whenever someone thinks about you, one of two things happen: You either call them or you pop up to see them."

I want to be perfectly clear: I have no doubt there are millions of people in this world who have a little voice that talks to them. But there are also people in this world who are gifted with having that sixth sense. I have experienced many things throughout my life that lead me to believe I am one of those gifted ones. As an adult I am much more in tune with the little voice and intuition than I was as a kid; but even saying that, there were times as a child when my sixth sense came through clear as a bell...

My grammar school was only a few blocks from my house, so I usually walked to school every morning. It was probably around late May, getting close to when school let out for the summer, and I was probably thinking about going down south to spend it at my grandparents' farm.

It was one of those perfect mornings where the day promised to be warm but not too hot; the sky was blue and a few white fluffy clouds floated around. Even the birds sang and hopped around. I only had a

The Stump

couple of blocks left before I got to school when my eye caught sight of a little kid in front of me, running and playing in the middle of the street, not a care in the world. He wasn't paying attention to anything, just content on having fun on this beautiful day.

I stopped dead in my tracks on the sidewalk. A sense of dread came over me, a dread so strong that I felt this little kid was in grave danger. I turned and looked behind me and saw a car barreling down the street coming up fast and heading straight for the boy. I don't know if the driver was drunk or what, but I did know the little boy was going to get hit.

Without a thought about what could possibly happen to me, I ran as fast as I could and launched myself at the little boy and hit him square in the chest. I pushed him, and with my momentum it sent him flying out of the way from the path of the car; likewise, my forward motion carried me out of the way and I rolled and hit the curb, just as the car sped past us.

The car didn't stop but kept on going. I jumped up and ran toward the little kid who had hit the curb just like I had. He was crying. I took him in my arms, looked at him, and turned him around this way and that, trying to see if he had been injured.

I held him at arm's length, looked at him, and said, "Are you okay? Are you hurt?"

He cried and cried. I embraced the little boy, held him as he shook, and then my whole body started to shake as well. For a few minutes that little boy and I shook together. The realization hit me that I could have died. Our shaking eventually subsided, he stopped crying, and I let the little kid go. The young boy looked at me and then a little smile came over his face. Before I knew it he took off and ran away. I got up and brushed myself off. I had a scrape on my arm; that was all there was left to remind me of what had happened. I continued on and went to school.

I didn't think much about it during the rest of the day, but I did tell my mom what had happened when I got home from school. She was concerned and asked me, "Are you okay?"

I replied, "Yeah, but I didn't expect anything like that to happen to me, Mom."

"What made you run out there like that?"

"I thought about that little kid. I didn't want him to get hit. It was strange because it felt like it wasn't me. I saw everything that happened but I was still on the sidewalk and it really wasn't me that did it; someone else ran out there, pushed him out of the way, and rolled to the curb. It all happened in just a matter of seconds, Mom, and there was no one around. Nobody to say, 'Did you see that?' No one to say, 'Oh my God, you're a hero!' I didn't think about any of that. All I knew was this young kid was about to get hit."

That experience might have been the catalyst that started me thinking about the whole notion of wanting to be part of something that was bigger than myself. If not me then who? If I hadn't helped that little boy, who else would have?

I'm not a guy who likes to do a lot of talking in the sense of when action needs to be done. I'm more of the doer type. There are people in this world who talk a lot, but they don't do a lot. Then there are people who do a heck of lot, but they don't have much to say.

I want to be someone who can say, "I made a difference." If it means I have to give up my life to do that, then so be it. That's one of the reasons why I knew I was meant to be a service member, destined to serve my country. I wanted to give back. I wanted to be part of something that was greater and bigger than myself. If it meant my life would be taken because of it, then at least I knew I went doing something I thought would make a difference.

I think even when I was little and I didn't know the exact meaning of the words or understood the speech, I do remember I sat and watched

The Stump

President Kennedy say the words, "And so my fellow Americans, I ask of you, ask not what your country can do for you, but ask what can you do for your country."*

I thought a lot about those words. It made sense to me. I asked myself, *What are you going to do for your country? This is your country regardless of how it is, no matter how bad or how much inequality there is in terms of how it treats you as an African American. What are you going to do to contribute? Every race has made contributions to our great nation over time. All you have to do is study history to realize that. So many have stepped up at one point in time or another to move this nation forward. To sit and only criticize, never lending your voice, action, or heart to a cause — I have little respect for those people. No matter how many issues we have in this country, we are a great democratic nation. We all have a voice, and we have it so much better than so many others in this world.*

My dad would sit and talk to my brother, sister, and me at the dinner table after supper was finished and the dishes washed and put away. I have fond memories of those family talks and remember more than once my mom having said, "Don't you know it's late? You guys have school tomorrow and you need to get to bed."

"Oh, Mom, just a little longer?"

"No, you need to get to bed."

My dad would add, "Your mom is right. There will be other days."

As we never argued with Mom or Dad, we obediently replied, "We love you," and off we would go to bed, excited about the next time we would all sit down together as a family.

We didn't have much in the material sense and we were definitely not rich, but we had one of the most powerful gifts that can be given to a family. We had love.

I heard about white kids that lived in big grand houses who were given new cars after they got their driver's license. Their dads and even sometimes their moms had high-paying jobs, and they belonged to the country club. We called them WASPs (White Anglo-Saxon Protestants). I used to wonder why these white kids ran away from home. Seemed to me they had everything: their own bedroom, probably their own bathroom, a new car to drive, clothes, money in their pockets, and the best schools, which meant they had a future. But you see, material things don't make a family happy, and even though they might have been wealthy, we were richer than they ever would be. We had love, and they didn't.

Many of my dad's conversations at the dinner table would be along the lines of "make your lives matter." He would turn directly at me and ask, "Son, why do you exist? You must find the reason why you matter. If you don't know why you exist or why you matter, then your life has no meaning. There has to be a reason why you are here, so find your purpose, make a difference, and make your life mean something."

Those evening talks at the dinner table helped define me as a young adolescent, a teenager, and finally as a man. It helped me shape my thoughts to understand that to define myself, I had to look at every part of who I was, and know I could be somebody of worth, so that I could respect myself and be respected by others. That single word *respect* means so much to an African American.

My dad would say, "Never take shortcuts. Always take the hard road. The hard road is the road that will get you the better life. Never be what I became. Be better!"

I told my dad, "But I like who you are, Dad. You're better than so many others."

"No, I'm simply a provider. I provide the best I can for my family, but I want you to be better. I want you to do better. I want you to have better. I want you to be better than I ever could be."

I watched him get up and go to work, on many occasions going in as sick as a dog. It hurt me to see him struggle. I asked Mom, "Why is he going to work? Why is he doing this? He's sick."

The Stump

My mom would say, "He wants to provide for all of you. He believes in this family, and all of you are his family now, regardless if you are not his biological son or your sister is not his biological daughter. It's his job to be the breadwinner of the family and provide for us. That's why he's doing what he does. He sees us as his responsibility and it's his way of being a contributor. That's why *his* life matters. Every parent wants the best for their kids. The ultimate goal for every parent, the good ones anyway, is to do the very best for their children and have them do better than they did. That's your dad's way of giving back."

Giving back. Those two little words had such a powerful impact on my life. Giving back wasn't always about giving to others; sometimes giving back and having that sixth sense and listening to it was also about giving back to myself...

During the Christmas holiday season, I, like a lot of other service members was excited about coming home for the holidays. On the morning I was scheduled to depart and headed out to the airport, I was held up in traffic. Something told me not to fly that day. I made my way out of traffic, stopped, and called the airlines to reschedule my flight. My original flight I was supposed to fly out on did not reach American soil. It blew up over Scotland.

Simple intuitions; nothing more than moving to the right instead of to the left, of opening that door instead of this door, of staying or going. I have never questioned it and have followed my sixth sense my whole life. It has served me well throughout all of my years. I know I am still here today because I have stopped, I have listened, and I have heeded the unspoken words that come with having — the sixth sense.

Chapter 15

FINAL THOUGHTS

"*If you want better, you have to do better.*" These were Mrs. Hannaberry's closing words to all of us as we prepared to find our place in American society. As we each took our turn and left the Stump, I knew I would take Mrs. Hannaberry's life lessons she taught to each of us, and her powerful words she had spoken to me, and I would always have them close at hand as I set out on my own. I knew the road and path I was on was not going to be easy, nor did I expect it to be. I did, however, feel prepared for the challenges that were to come.

I wanted to make a difference. My making a difference wasn't just about being patriotic and honoring our great country and our American flag. It wasn't just about honor, duty, integrity, and selfless service; of course these words are embodied inside of me.

I however also wanted to set an example and make a difference for other young African Americans who come from the ghetto streets of Chicago like me; and other American kids who come from ghettos that unfortunately exist throughout our nation who have been told "you can't," "no," or "you're not good enough."

For those who long and yearn for change, I want to give them courage, hope, and the knowledge and understanding that they can make it out. It's about human nature that has been given to us by the

The Stump

Almighty — the will to survive; that basic instinct that drives us as human beings to live. One of my pet peeves throughout my military career was hearing soldiers' excuses. I always countered with the simple words, "If a ghetto kid from the South Side of Chicago can make it out and make something of himself, then you don't have any excuse I want to hear."

Everyone has heard the saying "How bad do you want it?" If you want something bad enough and you are willing to work hard to achieve it, you can reach your goals. You have to believe in yourself and give it everything you've got. Put your heart, your mind, and your soul toward making your dreams come true. Nothing is impossible if you are willing to take the steps to accomplish it. If you have a setback, pick yourself up, dust yourself off, and press on.

Personally for me, one of the hardest parts in my early career was keeping my mouth shut, which was something I didn't always succeed at! However, I did have enough fortitude, most of the time, to endure and keep my mouth closed. It certainly would have been easier many times to just say, "The heck with you, to heck with the military, I'm going back to Chicago." I, however, didn't want to be the one who "came back," and I definitely didn't want to return to the Stump and see Mrs. Hannaberry and bring excuses back and disappoint her.

I took the opportunity to experience the big ocean she talked about so many years ago. I have traveled many roads throughout my career. Not all have blessed me with rewards, but all have come with opportunities. Those opportunities, missteps, and pain that I have encountered and endured have provided me with many learning experiences as I've gone along my journey. I have now dealt with the not-so-good memories, and with professional help, I have taken the items I had stored away in the Box and made peace with them.

I like to say, "Have a little faith and everything is going to be all right." That thought I've carried with me throughout my life and I've kept it close at hand during my military career. I have always been inspired by and thankful for having my grandmother in my life. She, most of all, influenced my faith. The words she spoke to me on that fateful day before the journey of her life ended had such an impact on me. I will always remember her words: "Whenever you have a problem, no matter how big or how small it is, I want you to give it to the Lord and leave it alone."

How could I know that my path to success that the Almighty would put me on would begin at the Stump? And oddly enough but more importantly, not returning back to the Stump, like so many others had done before me, would be even more important. It did not signify that I no longer had a yearning for the Stump; it signified something Mrs. Hannaberry wanted for all of us, especially for me.

She said, *"Terry, I know you can do better and I have always wanted better for you."*

I truly believe at that parting moment, Mrs. Hannaberry was telling me not to come back. Although I will carry the memories of the Stump with me forever, and it will always be a part of me for the rest of my life, I was given permission to leave.

With Mrs. Hannaberry's blessing and my faith, I made my way out.

NOTES

Duck and Cover

"Interracial marriage in the United States," Wikipedia, last modified April 12, 2017, https://en.wikipedia.org/wiki/Interracial_marriage_in_the_United_States.

The Greatest

"Muhammad Ali," Wikipedia, last modified January 23, 2017, https://en.wikipedia.org/wiki/Muhammad_Ali.

The Paper Route

DNAinfo Staff, "Chicago's Martin Luther King Jr. Drive: A Road Through History," last updated January 21, 2013, https://www.dnainfo.com/chicago/20130121/chicago/chicagos-martin-luther-king-jr-drive-road-through-history.

The Baseball Game

"Negro league baseball," Wikipedia, last modified December 13, 2016, https://en.wikipedia.org/wiki/Negro_league_baseball.

The Stump

Hanging Out

Condon, David. "Making of a prep champion, Hirsch high school's rise to the top," *Chicago Tribune*, March 30, 1973, http://archives.chicagotribune.com/1973/03/30/page/69/article/making-of-a-prep-champion.

Siegel, Donald. "Race and Sport, Chapter 3," accessed January 21, 2017, http://www.science.smith.edu/exer_sci/ESS200/Raceh/Race03.htm.

"Reel Life Wisdom, Danny DeVito," Copyright © 2017 Doug Manning, accessed January 16, 2017, http://www.reellifewisdom.com/taxonomy/term/danny_devito.

They Came Back

"Voices of Democracy: The U.S. Oratory Project, John Fitzgerald Kennedy, Inaugural Address (20 January 1961)," Copyright © Voices of Democracy.site: Academic Web Pages, accessed January 22, 2017, http://voicesofdemocracy.umd.edu/kennedy-inaugural-address-speech-text/.

The Sixth Sense

"Voices of Democracy: The U.S. Oratory Project, John Fitzgerald Kennedy, Inaugural Address (20 January 1961)," Copyright © Voices of Democracy.site: Academic Web Pages, accessed January 22, 2017, http://voicesofdemocracy.umd.edu/kennedy-inaugural-address-speech-text/.

www.ingramcontent.com/pod-product-compliance
Lightning Source LLC
Chambersburg PA
CBHW030453010526
44118CB00011B/912